Where I'm Reading From

ALSO BY TIM PARKS

Where I'm Reading From
The Changing World of Books

Tim Parks

NEW YORK REVIEW BOOKS

New York

THIS IS A NEW YORK REVIEW BOOK
PUBLISHED BY THE NEW YORK REVIEW OF BOOKS
435 Hudson Street, New York NY 10014
www.nyrb.com

Library of Congress Cataloging-in-Publication Data

Parks, Tim.
Where I'm reading from : the changing world of books / by Tim Parks.
pages cm.—(New York Review Books Collections)
ISBN 978-1-59017-884-3 (hardback)
1. Books and reading. 2. Fiction. 3. Authorship. I. Title.
Z1003.P236 2015
028'.9—dc23

2014040981

ISBN 978-1-59017-884-3
Available as an electronic book; ISBN 978-1-59017-885-0

Printed in the United States of America on acid-free paper
1 3 5 7 9 10 8 6 4 2

Contents

Acknowledgments

I'D JUST LIKE to thank everybody who made this book what it is. Above all Hugh Eakin for all his thoughtful input and editing on every single piece, then Robert Silvers of course, Rea Hederman, Gabriel Winslow-Yost, and all the team at *The New York Review of Books*. Books are a joint effort. Many many thanks.

Introduction

IT'S TIME TO rethink everything. Everything. What it means to write and what it means to write for a public—and which public. What do I want from this writing? Money? A career? Recognition? A place in the community? A change in the government? World peace? Is it an artifice, is it therapy? Is it therapy *because* it is an artifice, or in spite of that? Does it have to do with constructing an identity, a position in society? Or simply with entertaining myself, with entertaining others? Will I still write if they don't pay me?

And what does it mean to read? Do I want to read the things other people are reading, so I can talk to them? Which other people? Why do I want to talk to them? So that I can be *of my time*? Or so that I can know other times, other places? Do I read things to confirm my vision of the world, or to challenge it? Or is reading to challenge my vision a reassuring confirmation that I am indeed the courageous guy I thought I was? The more challenging the books I read the more complacent I feel.

Does the idea of one world, one culture, mean we are all being driven toward the same books—in which case how many writers can there possibly be? Or will everyone be a writer, but without being paid? "No one can do without some semblance of immortality," remarked Emil Cioran. "Ever since death came to be accepted as the absolute end, *everybody writes*!"

Why do we so often disagree about the books we read? Is it because someone's reading well and someone's reading badly? The professor and the students? Because there are good books and bad, or because people with different backgrounds inevitably like different books? If so, can we begin to predict who will like what?

Most book talk is formulaic and has been for decades. Your average review offers a quick value judgment summed up in one-to-five stars at the top of the column. Why read on? There'll be a declaration of theme (worthy), an assessment of narrative competence, some mention of character and setting (we've all done a creative writing course), some praise, some reservations. Above all it's understood that books are introduced into a fierce competition for what few crumbs of celebrity TV and film have left to them. They have to hit the ground running. Toward the end there may or may not be a precious quote the publisher can use for the cover of the paperback edition. In 99.9 percent of cases the reviewer knows perfectly well what books are for, why they are written and read, what's literature and what's genre. He's ticking boxes. Or she. Understandably, the newspapers have reduced the books section to the size of a postage stamp.

For feedback there's the Internet. Sometime it feels like all feedback and no feed. What's most surprising on sites where readers offer their own reviews is how similar they are to journalistic reviews. They don't object to distributing the Amazon stars. They know perfectly well how to hand out praise and punishment. They have their unquestioned criteria. The medium dictates the tone. "I haven't actually read the book, but..."

In the weeklies that still cover books, the author interview comes in the form of the same ten questions for all. "When did you last cry?"

"What is your greatest regret?" It's an invitation to look for distinction in quirkiness. Usually by email. "Of the novels you've written, which is your favorite?" "What are you reading now, during the day and at bedtime?" Apparently interviewers know that all authors read different things at bedtime. They are not allowed not to have a favorite novel, a greatest regret. The small photo running beside the piece is taken from the author's Facebook page at no expense to the paper.

The multiplication of literary prizes is in line with this. Their uncoupling from national literatures tells us that it's the reputation of the prize that counts, not nurturing writers in a given community. People have invested money. The longlist is added to the shortlist to squeeze out a little more publicity. At the awards dinner, one writer is hoisted up to the pantheon and the others cast off into outer darkness. It doesn't matter that the winner was no one's first choice, that two members of the jury complained they couldn't finish the damn book. It's a winner now. By democratic process. And the winner's sales outstrip the loser's, the losers'.

Meantime literary scholarship in the universities is impenetrable: less monumentally abstruse perhaps than in the rarefied heyday of structuralism and post-structuralism, but maybe that's because there's no need to work so hard not to be read these days. The tired jargon is enough, the tendency to confuse studies of literature with exercises in cultural history. It is astonishing how many hundreds of thousands of academic articles are produced to no end aside from the conferring of this or that teaching contract, how much endeavor and how little adventure.

Beneath all the chatter and the liturgy runs a fierce nostalgia for the literary myths of the past, for the gigantic figures of Dickens and Joyce, Hemingway and Faulkner. A writer can't even aim at that kind of aura today. But it's that yearning for imagined greatness that drives the whole literary enterprise. Plus the publishers' desperation to manufacture a bestseller to pay the bills. The idea of greatness is a marketing tool. See Franzen.

Perhaps in the end it's just ridiculous, the high opinion we have of books, of literature. Perhaps it's just a collective spell of self-regard, self-congratulation, the way the jurors of the literary prize are so damn pleased with themselves when they invite their new hero to the podium. Do books, after all, *change* anything? For all their proverbial liberalism, have they made the world more liberal? Or have they offered the fig leaf that allows us to go on as we were, liberal in our reading and conservative in our living. Perhaps art is more part of the problem than the solution; we may be going to hell, but look how well we write about it, look at our paintings and operas and tragedies.

It is not, after all, that we have to worry about the survival of literature. There's never been so much of it. But maybe it's time that the beast carried a health warning.

—Milan, May 2014

NB: Impersonal use of the third-person pronoun has become a problem for the contemporary writer in English. People have grown sensitive to issues of gender. Do I say, "Someone who has been told he is dying and must make his will..." or "Someone who has been told he or she is dying and must make his or her will"? My own feeling is that the old "he" was always understood to be impersonal and without gender while the he-or-she formula is fussy and inelegant, constantly reminding readers of a problem that isn't really there. For the most part then, I have stayed with the old impersonal *he* and I invite my readers to believe that I do not do this in a spirit of chauvinism, but to keep the focus sharp.

I

The World Around the Book

DO WE NEED STORIES?

LET'S TACKLE ONE of the literary set's favorite orthodoxies head on: that the world "needs" stories. "There is an enormous need," Jonathan Franzen declares in an interview with *Corriere della Sera* (there's no escape these days), "for long, elaborate, complex stories, such as can only be written by an author concentrating alone, free from the deafening chatter of Twitter."

Of course as a novelist it is convenient to think that by the nature of the job one is on the side of the good, supplying an urgent and general need. I can also imagine readers drawing comfort from the idea that their fiction habit is essential sustenance and not a luxury. But what is the nature of this need? What would happen if it wasn't met? We might also ask: Why does Franzen refer to *complex* stories? And why is it important not to be interrupted by Twitter and Facebook? Are such interruptions any worse than an old landline phone call, or simply friends and family buzzing around your writing table? Jane Austen, we recall, loved to write in domestic spaces where she was open to constant interruption.

Proponents of the-world-needs-stories thesis are legion, but one of the more elaborate statements comes in Salman Rushdie's novel

Haroun and the Sea of Stories (1990). Here, in a text that falls between fable and magical realism, the telling of many stories is aligned with the idea of a natural ecology; in the normal and healthy way of things, we're told, all the different stories of the world flow together in a great ocean of narrative. But now this harmony is threatened by an evil "cultmaster" who seeks to poison and eventually shut off the flow of stories, imposing universal silence and sterility as part of a bid for omnipotence.

Given Rushdie's personal plight at the time of writing, it's hard not to think of the "cultmaster" as a metamorphosis of the Ayatollah Khomeini. Stories are presented as a manifestation of the natural pluralism of the imagination, engaged in a mortal battle against any fundamentalism that would impose its own, univocal version: fiction is on the side of freedom. Of course.

Rushdie's idea is charming, but his ocean-of-stories argument never, to risk a pun, holds water. Far from flowing together in a harmonious ecology, stories tend to be in constant competition with each other. Far from imposing silence, cults, religions, and ideologies all have their own noisy stories to tell. Christian fundamentalism with its virgin birth, miracles, exorcisms, and angels boasts a rich narrative flora; if we toss into the mix the Catholic saints and their colorful martyrdoms, we can hardly complain that the censorship and repression of the Inquisition resulted in storyless silence.

Rather the problem is that preacher and polemicist want us to accept just one, exclusive set of stories, one vision, which we must believe is true. And many people are happy to do this. Once they've signed up to a Christian, Muslim, Buddhist, or even liberal pluralist narrative, it's unlikely they'll go out of their way to research competing accounts of the world. People tend to use stories of whatever kind to bolster their beliefs, not to question them.

But I doubt if this politicized version of the we-need-stories thesis was what a writer like Franzen had in mind. "This is an excellent novel," I remember a fellow judge for a literary prize repeatedly telling the rest of the jury every time he encouraged us to vote for a book, "because it offers complex moral situations that help us get a sense of how to live and behave." The argument here is that the world has become immensely complicated and the complex stories of novels help us to see our way through it, to shape a trajectory for ourselves in the increasingly fragmented and ill-defined social environment we move in.

There's something to be said for this idea, though of course stories are by no means the exclusive territory of novels; the political, sports, and crime pages of the newspapers are full of fascinating stories, many of them extremely challenging and complex. What the novel offers, however, is a tale mediated by the individual writer, who (alone, away from Facebook and Twitter) works hard to shape it and deliver it in a way that he or she feels is especially attractive, compelling, and right.

Here again, though, even if we are not immediately aware of it, and even when the author is celebrated for his or her *elusive ambiguity* (another lit-crit commonplace), such stories compete for our assent and seek to seduce us toward the author's point of view. D. H. Lawrence attacked Tolstoy's novels as evil, immoral, and deeply corrupting. Writing about Thomas Hardy, he rather brilliantly questions the motives behind Hardy's habit of having his more talented and spiritually adventurous characters destroyed by society; Hardy goes "against himself," Lawrence tells us (meaning, against his own specially gifted nature), to "stand with the average against the exception," and all this "in order to explain his own sense of failure." To Lawrence's mind, a tremendously complex story like *Jude the Obscure* becomes an invitation not to try to realize your full potential but to settle instead for self-preservation. Hardy reinforces the mental habits of the frightened reader. It is pernicious. In this view of things, rather than needing stories, we need to learn how to smell out their drift and resist them.

But there's something deeper going on. Even before we actually tell any stories, the language we use teems with them in embryo form. There are words that simply denote things in nature: a pebble, a tree. There are words that describe objects we make: to know the word *chair* is to understand about moving from standing to sitting and appreciate the match of the human body with certain shapes and materials. But there are also words that come complete with entire narratives, or rather that can't come without them. The only way we can understand words like *God, angel, devil, ghost* is through stories, since these entities do not allow themselves to be known in other ways, or not to the likes of me. Here not only is the word invented— all words are—but the *referent* is invented too, and a story to suit. God is a one-word creation story.

Arguably the most important word in the invented-referents category is *self.* We would like the self to exist perhaps, but does it really? What is it? The need to surround it with a lexical cluster of reinforcing terms—identity, character, personality, soul—all with equally dubious referents suggests our anxiety. The more words we invent, the more we feel reassured that there really is something there to refer to.

Like God, the self requires a story; it is the account of how each of us accrues and sheds attributes over seventy or eighty years—youth, vigor, job, spouse, success, failure—while remaining, at some deep level, myself, my soul. One of the accomplishments of the novel, which as we know blossomed with the consolidation of Western individualism, has been to reinforce this ingenious invention, to have us believe more and more strongly in this sovereign self whose essential identity remains unchanged by all vicissitudes. Telling the stories of various characters in relation to each other, how something started, how it developed, how it ended, novels are intimately involved with the way we make up ourselves. They reinforce a process we are engaged in every moment of the day, self creation. They sustain the idea of a self projected through time, a self eager to be a real something (even at the cost of great suffering) and not an illusion.

The more complex and historically dense the stories are, the stronger the impression they give of unique and protracted individual identity beneath surface transformations, conversions, dilemmas, aberrations. In this sense, even pessimistic novels—say, J. M. Coetzee's *Disgrace*—can be encouraging: however hard circumstances may be, you do have a self, a personal story to shape and live. You are a unique something that can fight back against all the confusion around. You have pathos.

This is all perfectly respectable. But do we actually *need* this intensification of self that novels provide? Do we need it more than ever before?

I suspect not. If we asked the question of, for example, a Buddhist priest, he or she would probably tell us that it is precisely this illusion of selfhood that makes so many in the West unhappy. We are in thrall to the narrative of selves that do not really exist, a fabrication in which most novel-writing connives. Schopenhauer would have agreed. He spoke of people "deluded into an absolutely false view of life by reading novels," something that "generally has the most harmful effect on their whole lives." Like the Buddhist priest, he would have preferred silence or the school of experience, or the kind of myth or fable that did not invite excited identification with an author alter ego.

Personally, I'm too enmired in narrative and self-narrative to bail out now. I love an engaging novel, I love a complex novel; but I am quite sure I don't *need* it.

WHY FINISH BOOKS?

"SIR—" REMARKED SAMUEL JOHNSON with droll incredulity to someone too eager to know whether he had finished a certain book—"Sir, do you read books through?" Well, do we? Right through to the end? And if we do, are we the suckers Johnson supposed us to be?

Schopenhauer, who thought and wrote a great deal about reading, is on Johnson's side. Life is "too short for bad books" and "a few pages" should be quite enough, he claims, for "a provisional estimate of an author's productions." After which it is perfectly okay to put an author back on the shelf if you're not convinced.

But I'm not really interested in how we deal with bad books. It seems obvious that any serious reader will have learned long ago how much time to give a book before choosing to shut it. It's only the young, still attached to that sense of achievement inculcated by anxious parents, who hang on doggedly when there is no enjoyment. "I'm a teenager," remarks one sad contributor to a book review website:

> I read this whole book [it would be unfair to say which] from
> first page to last hoping it would be as good as the reviews said.
> It wasn't. I enjoy reading and finish nearly all the novels I start

and it was my determination never to give up that made me finish this one, but I really wish I hadn't.

One can only encourage a reader like this to learn not to attach self-esteem to the mere finishing of a book, if only because the more bad books you finish, the fewer good ones you'll have time to start.

What about those good books, though? Because Johnson certainly wasn't just referring to the bad when he tossed out that provocation. Do we need to finish them? Is a good book by definition one that we did finish? Or are there occasions when we might choose to leave off a book before the end, or even only halfway through, and nevertheless feel that it was good, even excellent, that we were glad we read what we read, but don't feel the need to finish it? I ask the question because this is happening to me more and more often. Is it age, wisdom, senility? I start a book. I'm enjoying it thoroughly, and then the moment comes when I just know I've had enough. It's not that I've stopped enjoying it. I'm not bored, I don't even think it's too long. I just have no desire to go on enjoying it. Can I say then that I've read it? Can I recommend it to others and speak of it as a fine book?

Kafka remarked that beyond a certain point, a writer might decide to finish his or her novel at any moment, with any sentence; it really was an arbitrary question, like where to cut a piece of string, and in fact both *The Castle* and *America* are left unfinished, while *The Trial* is tidied away with the indecent haste of someone who has decided enough is enough. The Italian novelist Carlo Emilio Gadda was the same; both his major works, *That Awful Mess on the Via Merulana* and *Acquainted with Grief,* are unfinished and both are considered classics despite the fact that they have complex plots that would seem to require endings that are not there.

Other writers deploy what I would call a catharsis of exhaustion:

their books present themselves as rich and extremely taxing experiences that simply come to an end at some point where writer, reader, and indeed characters all feel they've had enough. The earliest example that comes to mind is D. H. Lawrence, but one thinks of Elfriede Jelinek, Thomas Bernhard, Samuel Beckett, and the wonderful Christina Stead. Beckett's prose fiction gets shorter and shorter, denser and denser as he brings the point of exhaustion further and further forward.

All these writers it seems to me, by suggesting that beyond a certain point a book might end anywhere, legitimize the notion that the reader may choose for him or herself where to bow out (of Proust's *Recherche* for example, or Mann's *Magic Mountain*) without detracting anything from the experience. One of the strangest responses I ever had to a novel of my own—my longest not surprisingly—came from a fellow author who wrote out of the blue to express his appreciation. Such letters of course are a massive boost to one's vanity, and I was just about to stick this very welcome feather in my cap, when I reached the last lines of the message: he hadn't read the last fifty pages, he said, because he'd reached a point where the novel seemed satisfactorily over.

Naturally I was disappointed, even a little angry. My leg had surely been pulled. Wasn't this damning criticism, that I'd gone on fifty pages too long? Only later did I appreciate his candor. My book was fine, for him, even without the ending. It wasn't too long, just that he was happy to stop where he did.

What, then, since clearly I'm talking about books with aesthetic pretensions, of the notion of the work of art as an organic whole— you haven't seen its shape unless you've seen all of it? And, since again I have mainly referred to novelists, what of the question of plot? A novel that is plotted requires that we reach the end, because the solution to the tale will throw meaning back across the entire work. So the critics tell us. No doubt I've made this claim myself in some review or other.

But this is not really my experience as I read. There are some novels, and not just genre novels, where plot is indeed up front and very much the reason why one keeps turning the pages. We have to know what happens. These are rarely the most important books for me. Often one skims as heightened engagement with the plot reduces our attention to the writing as such; all the novel's intelligence is in the story and the writing the merest vehicle.

Yet even in these novels where plot is the central pleasure on offer, the end rarely gratifies, and if we like the book and recommend it to others, it is rarely for the end. What matters is the conundrum of the plot, the forces put in play and the tensions between them. The Italians have a nice word here. They call plot *trama*, a word whose primary meaning is weft, woof, or weave. It is the pattern of the weave that we most savor in a plot—Hamlet's dilemma, perhaps, or the awesome unsustainability of Dorothea's marriage to Casaubon—not its solution. Indeed, the best we can hope from the end of a good plot is that it not ruin what came before. I would not mind a Hamlet that stopped before the carnival of carnage in the last scene, leaving us instead to mull over all the intriguing possibilities posed by the young prince's return to Elsinore.

In this regard it's worth noting that stories were not always obliged to have an end, or to keep the same ending. In *The Marriage of Cadmus and Harmony*, Roberto Calasso shows that one of the defining characteristics of a living mythology is that its many stories, so excitingly tangled together, always have at least two endings, often "opposites"—the hero dies, he doesn't die, the lovers marry, they don't marry. It was only when myth became history, as it were, that we began to feel there should be just one "proper" version, and set about forgetting the alternatives. With novels, the endings I'm least disappointed with are those that encourage the reader to believe that the story might very easily have taken a completely different turn.

To put a novel down before the end, then, is simply to acknowledge that for me its shape, its aesthetic quality, is in the weave of the plot and, with the best novels, in the meshing of the writing style with that weave. Style and plot, overall vision and local detail, fascinate together, in a perfect tangle. Once the structure has been set up and the narrative ball is rolling, the need for an end is just an unfortunate burden, an embarrassment, a deplorable closure of so much possibility. Sometimes I have experienced the fifty pages of suspense that so many writers feel condemned to close with as a stretch of psychological torture, obliging me to think of life as a machine for manufacturing pathos and tragedy, since the only endings we halfway believe in, of course, are the unhappy ones.

I wonder if, when a bard was recounting a myth, after some early Athenian dinner party perhaps, or round some campfire on the Norwegian coast, there didn't come a point when listeners would vote to decide which ending they wanted to hear, or simply opt for an early bed. In our own times, Alan Ayckbourn has written plays with different endings, in which the cast decides, act by act, which version they will follow.

Might it be that, in showing a willingness not to pursue even an excellent book to the death, you are actually doing the writer a favor, exonerating him or her from the near impossible task of getting out of the plot gracefully? There is a tyranny about our thrall to endings. I don't doubt I would have a lower opinion of many of the novels I haven't finished if I had. Perhaps it is time that I learned, in my own novels, to drop readers a hint or two that, from this or that moment on, they have my permission to let the book go just as and when they choose.

E-BOOKS ARE FOR GROWN-UPS

INTERVIEWED AFTER WINNING the Costa Prize for Literature, the distinguished British novelist Andrew Miller remarked that while he assumed that soon most popular fiction would be read on screen, he believed and hoped that literary fiction would continue to be read on paper. In his 2011 Man Booker Prize acceptance speech, Julian Barnes made his own plea for the survival of printed books. At the university where I work, certain professors, old and young, will react with vehement disapproval at the notion that one is reading poetry on a Kindle. It is sacrilege.

Are they right?

In practical terms it is all too easy to defend the e-book. We can buy a text instantly wherever we are in the world. We pay less. We use no paper, occupy no space. Kindle's wireless system keeps our page, even when we open the book on a different reader than the one on which we left off. We can change the type size according to the light and our eyesight. We can change the font according to our taste. Cooped up in the press of the metro, we turn the pages by applying a light pressure of the thumb. Lying in bed, we don't have that problem of having to use two hands to keep a fat paperback open.

But I want to go beyond practicality to the reading experience itself, our engagement with the text. What is it that these literary men and women are afraid of losing should the paper novel really go into decline? Surely not the cover, so often a repository of misleading images and tediously fulsome endorsements. Surely not the pleasure of running fingers and eyes over fine paper, something that hardly alters whether one is reading Jane Austen or Dan Brown. Hopefully it is not the quality of the paper that determines our appreciation for the classics.

Could it be the fact that the e-book thwarts our ability to find particular lines by remembering their position on the page? Or our love of scribbling comments (of praise and disgust) in the margin? It's true that on first engagement with the e-book, we become aware of all kinds of habits that are no longer possible, skills developed over many years that are no longer relevant. We can't so easily flick through the pages to see where the present chapter ends, or whether so and so is going to die now or later. In general, the e-book discourages browsing, and though the bar at the bottom of the screen showing the percentage of the book we've completed lets us know more or less where we're up to, we don't have the reassuring sense of the physical weight of the thing (how proud children are when they get through their first long tome!), nor the computational pleasures of page numbers (Dad, I read fifty pages today). This can be a problem for academics: it's hard to give a proper reference if you don't have page numbers.

But are these old habits essential? Mightn't they actually be distracting us from the written word itself? Weren't there perhaps specific pleasures when reading on parchment scroll that we know nothing of and have lived happily without? Certainly there were those who lamented the loss of calligraphy when the printing press made type impersonal. There were some who believed that serious readers would always prefer serious books to be copied by hand.

What are the core characteristics of literature as a medium and an art form? Unlike painting there is no physical image to contemplate, nothing that impresses itself on the eye in the same way, given equal eyesight. Unlike sculpture, there is no artifact you can walk around and touch. You don't have to travel to look at literature. You don't have to line up or stand in the crowd, or worry about getting a good seat. Unlike music you don't have to respect its timing, accepting an experience of a fixed duration. You can't dance to it or sing along or take a photo or make a video with your phone.

Literature is made up of words. They can be spoken or written. If spoken, volume and speed and accent can vary. If written, the words can appear in this or that typeface on any material, with any impagination. Joyce is as much Joyce in Baskerville as in Times New Roman. And we can read these words at any speed, interrupt our reading as frequently as we choose. Somebody who reads *Ulysses* in two weeks hasn't read it any more or less than someone who reads it in three months, or three years.

Only the sequence of the words must remain inviolate. We can change everything about a text but the words themselves and the order they appear in. The literary experience does not lie in any one moment of perception, or any physical contact with a material object (even less in the "possession" of handsome masterpieces lined up on our bookshelves), but in the movement of the mind through a sequence of words from beginning to end. More than any other art form it is pure mental material, as close as one can get to thought itself. Memorized, a poem is as surely a piece of literature in our minds as it is on the page. If we say the words in sequence, even silently without opening our mouths, then we have had a literary experience—perhaps even a more intense one than when we read them on the page. It's true that our owning the object—*War and Peace* or *Moby-Dick*—and organizing these and other classics according to chronology and nation of origin will give us an illusion of control: as if we had now "acquired" and "digested" and "placed" a piece of culture. Perhaps that is what people are attached to. But in fact we all know that once the sequence of words is over and the book closed what actually remains in our possession is very difficult, wonderfully difficult to pin down, a richness (or sometimes irritation) that has nothing to do with the heavy block of paper on our shelves.

The e-book, by eliminating all variations in the appearance and weight of the material object we hold in our hand and by discouraging anything but our focus on where we are in the sequence of words (the page once read disappears, the page to come has yet to appear) would seem to bring us closer than the paper book to the essence of the literary experience. Certainly it offers a more austere, direct engagement with the words appearing before us and disappearing behind us than the traditional paper book offers, giving no fetishistic gratification as we cover our walls with famous names. It is as if one had been freed from everything extraneous and distracting surrounding the text to focus on the pleasure of the words themselves. In this sense the passage from paper to e-book is not unlike the moment when we passed from illustrated children's books to the adult version of the page that is only text. This is a medium for grown-ups.

DOES COPYRIGHT MATTER?

DO I, AS an author, have the right to prevent people copying my books for free? Should I have it? Does it matter?

"They have taken away my right to own a slave," wrote Max Stirner, the opening words of the chapter on human rights in his great book, *The Ego and its Own* (1844). One paradoxical sentence to remind us that what we call rights are no more than what the law concedes to one party or another in any given conflict of interest. There are no rights in nature, only in a society with a legal system and a police force. Rights can be different in different countries, they may be notional or enforced.

Copyright, then, is part of a mass of legislation that governs the relationship between individual and collective, for the most part defending the former against the latter. You will only have copyright in a society that places a very high value on the individual, the individual intellect, the products of individual intellect. In fact, the introduction of a law of copyright is one of the signs of a passage from a hierarchical and holistic vision of society, to one based on the hopes and aspirations of the individual. Not surprisingly, the first legal moves toward creating the concept of copyright came in late-seventeenth-century Britain.

Officially the idea is that the writer, artist, or musician should be allowed to reap the just rewards for his effort. This is quaint. There is very little justice in the returns artists receive. Works of equal value and quality produce quite different incomes or no income at all. Somebody becomes a millionaire overnight and someone else cannot even publish. It is perfectly possible that the quality of work by these two writers is very similar. The same book may have a quite different fate in different countries. Any notion of justice in the incomes of artists is naive.

What we are talking about, more brutally, is preventing other people from making money from my work without paying me a tribute, because my work belongs to me. It's mine. What we are talking about is ownership and control. The law, as it now stands, concedes that I own what I write and hence have the right to keep track of every copy of the book I have published and to demand a percentage of the sale price. This right is the same whether I sell two hundred copies of the book at a local newsstand over some years, or twenty million over five continents in eighteen months.

And I can pass this ownership on to my children or heirs when I die; they inherit the right to collect royalties on every copy of my work made and sold, as if they had inherited a company or a property I was renting out. But only for seventy years. Having conceded so much to the individual, and then to his or her family, society finally denies that intellectual property is the same as physical property. My heirs can own my house forever, but at a certain point the product of my mind will be turned over to the public domain. The official rationale here is that I have made enough, and society, in order to build up and enjoy a shared culture, encouraging the accumulation of collective wisdom, needs to have free access to the products of my intellect, in much the same way as it has gained access to many of the great art collections and country estates of the rich men of the past.

We all sense that there is more instinct than logic at work here. We simply feel that it would be bizarre to be taking royalties from the work of an ancestor who lived four hundred years ago. It would be bizarre not to be able to quote Shakespeare without paying something to his descendants, if there are any. At the same time we do not feel that if we owned a painting an ancestor made and left to the family we should not have the right to keep it or to sell it for any price the market will offer.

In the recent past the duration of copyright after an author's death was extended from fifty to seventy years. We sense at once that a decision like this is arbitrary and could easily change again. Was it really necessary that James Joyce's grandson could charge more or less what he liked for quotations of the author's work, even in academic books, up to sixty-nine years after his death? Does it make sense that to quote three or four lines from *The Four Quartets* in a book about meditation I have to pay T. S. Eliot's estate £200? One feels the authors themselves might have rebelled, which gives us an insight into the real reason why works are allowed to go out of copyright protection. Because the author would have wished it thus. Once the immediate family has been protected, availability and celebrity is more important to an author than a revenue stream for descendants he has never met. The lapse of copyright is a concession to the author's dreams of immortality at the expense of the family.

Copyright has always been contested and hard to police, suggesting that there has never been a profound consensus about its ethical rectitude. Dickens, Lawrence, Joyce, and hosts of lesser authors all fought against pirated editions of their work. In the twentieth century, the opening of an international market for books and the progress in copying technology has exacerbated the problem. Can one really expect all countries to defend the rights of foreign authors, when the majority of international bestsellers come from half a dozen countries and overwhelmingly from the United States? Nor has copyright crime generally been "felt" in the same way as straightforward theft or burglary; I have never heard of copyright pirates afflicted by feelings of guilt and remorse. To make the situation more unstable, the combined innovations of the Internet and the e-book have not only introduced new ways of copying books, but also created a feeling, at least in some quarters, that all books should be freely available and consultable through my laptop or iPhone. There is a growing sense that copyright enforcement could become impossible.

To see how copyright law may survive, we have to ask, beyond the pieties and legal niceties, what its real social function is and whether there is at least a large constituency in favor of that function continuing. Copyright gives the writer a considerable financial incentive and locks his work into the world of money; each book becomes a lottery ticket. Huge sales will mean a huge income. Copyright thus encourages a novelist to direct his work not to his immediate peer group, those whose approval he most craves, but to the widest possible audience in possession of the price of a paperback.

On the one hand, then, by conceding copyright, society declares that it holds individual creativity in high esteem—every member of society can dream of one day benefiting from copyright, of transforming genius into money—but by the same token it draws the author into a bourgeois mentality where writing is a job with an income; the writer now has an investment in stable markets and attentive policing. In short, copyright keeps the writer in the polis, and indeed it is remarkable how little creative writing today is truly revolutionary, in the sense of seeking a profoundly different model for society. There is a subversive writerly attitude, of course—liberal, anti-authoritarian—which has paradoxically become almost a convention; dissatisfaction with society is expected of an author. All the same with a royalty check whose arrival relies on international agreements, electronic funds transfer, and a willingness to prosecute copyright piracy, he or she is more a creature of the status quo than its enemy. Perhaps this is a good thing. Perhaps it is limiting. Perhaps good things are inevitably limiting.

Imagine copyright were phased out or became impossible to enforce in any meaningful way: you can't expect an advance from a publisher, you can't even sell your work directly to readers online. So, creative writing is no longer a "job." You won't be able to turn it into a living unless you become a big-time celebrity, in which case no doubt there would be lucrative spin-offs; but celebrity is always a long shot and how will it be achieved if the ordinary commercial channels disappear? Isn't today's celebrity mostly constructed on sales, which are largely generated by hype, and which would evaporate if a publisher no longer had an exclusive right to publish a given book—or if a publisher could no longer charge the prices necessary to support the publicity required to get a book to its intended public? It's true that a certain buzz can now be created around a book simply by making it freely available on the net, as was the case with *Fifty Shades of Grey*; but that would be of little help if there were no prospect of turning that excitement into publishing support and money.

How would this situation change the way a writer works? Would it make sense now to write the thriller, literary or otherwise, that was once packaged and sold to entertain and to earn? Would I really want to write all those pages, if there wasn't even the chance of an income? Maybe yes. There is fan fiction after all. But many writers would not. "No man but a blockhead ever wrote, except for money," Samuel Johnson once remarked. I'm not with him 100 percent, but I know where he's coming from. One sees here the difference from the music industry: unable to police their copyright on CDs, musicians nevertheless go on writing songs and can enjoy the feedback and hopefully some income from performing them to an appreciative public; if the songs happen to catch on through the Internet then the musicians can enjoy notoriety and expect bigger concerts, if not a huge income from selling albums. But there is no such performance possibility for the prose thriller, or even the great American novel. Without the prospect of money, the author would have to think very hard about what he really wants to write and how he plans to engage with an eventual community of readers whose appreciation, if not cash, must suffice to give him the gratification and encouragement he seeks. In short, you wouldn't launch blindly into a major novel, as so many young writers do, simply because novels are the form that command attention and promise an income.

As soon as we put it like this, as soon as we imagine, or try to imagine, the extraordinary confusion, creative and otherwise, that might occur, the many and fragmented ways people might enjoy and share and despair of putting together reflections and entertainments in words for each other, you can see that it is not going to happen. There is still an enormous demand for the long traditional novel, for works that reinforce the idea of an individual whose identity is projected through time and who achieves some kind of wisdom or happiness through many vicissitudes. There is simply no form of escapism, mental immersion, or sustained illusion quite like the thousand-page fantasy narrative, whether it be the endless Harry Potters or the *Millennium* trilogy; if to have that experience we have to guarantee a substantial income to its creator then society will continue to find a way to do that, in the same way European soccer clubs still find ways to pay exorbitant salaries to their star players.

Copyright, we see, is not essentially driven by notions of justice or theories of ownership, but by a certain culture's attachment to a certain literary form. If people only read poetry, which you can never stop poets producing even when you pay them nothing at all, then the law of copyright would disappear in a trice.

THE DULL NEW GLOBAL NOVEL

NOT ALL WRITERS share the same sense of whom they are writing for. Many may not even think they are directing their work at any audience in particular. All the same, there are clearly periods of history when, across the board, authors' perceptions of who their readers are change, something that inevitably leads to a change in the kind of texts they produce. The most obvious example is the period that stretches from the fourteenth to the sixteenth century when writers all over Europe abandoned Latin for the vernacular. Instead of introducing their work, as before, into an international arena presided over by a largely clerical elite, they "descended" to local and national languages to address themselves to an emerging middle class.

In the history books this shift to the vernacular tends to be presented as a democratic inspiration that allowed a wealth of local vitality into the written text and brought new confidence to the rapidly consolidating national languages. That said, it was probably driven as much by ambition and economic interest as by idealism. There came a point when it no longer made sense to write in Latin because the arbiters of taste were now a national rather than international grouping. Today we are at the beginning of a revolution of even greater import that is taking us in a quite different direction.

As a result of rapidly accelerating globalization we are moving toward a world market for literature. There is a growing sense that for an author to be considered "great," he or she must be an international rather than a national phenomenon. This change is not perhaps as immediately evident in the US as it is in Europe, thanks to the size and power of the US market and the fact that English is generally perceived as the language of globalization, so that many more translations go out of English rather than into it. However, more and more European, African, Asian and South American authors see themselves as having "failed" if they do not reach an international audience.

In recent years authors in Germany, France, and Italy—all countries with large and well-established national readerships—have expressed to me their disappointment at not having found an English-language publisher for their works; interestingly, they complain that this failure reflects back on their prestige in their home country: if people don't want you elsewhere, you can't be that good. Certainly, in Italy where I live, an author is only thought to have arrived when he is published in New York. To appreciate how much things have changed one only need reflect that the reputations of writers like Zola or Verga would not have been dented at all by a failure to achieve publication in London.

This development has been hugely accelerated by electronic text transmission. Today, no sooner is a novel or even an opening chapter complete, than it can be submitted to scores of publishers all over the world. It is not unusual for foreign rights to be sold before the work has a local publisher. An astute agent can then orchestrate the simultaneous launch of a work in many different countries using promotional strategies that we normally associate with multinational corporations. Thus a reader picking up a copy of Dan Brown's *The Lost Symbol,* or the latest Harry Potter, or indeed a work by Umberto Eco, or Haruki Murakami, or Ian McEwan, does so in the knowledge that this same work is being read now, all over the world. Buying the book, a reader becomes part of an international community. This perception adds to the book's attraction.

The proliferation of international literary prizes has guaranteed that the phenomenon is not restricted to the more popular sector of the market. Despite its questionable selection procedures and often bizarre choices, the Nobel is seen as more important than any national prize. Meanwhile, the International IMPAC in Ireland, Premio Mondello in Italy, and the International Literature Award in Germany—prizes aimed at "international" literature rather than works from the country in question—are rapidly growing in prestige. Thus the arbiters of taste are no longer one's own compatriots—they are less easily knowable, not a group the author himself is part of.

What are the consequences for literature? From the moment an author perceives his ultimate audience as international rather than national, the nature of his writing is bound to change. In particular one notes a tendency to remove obstacles to international comprehension. Writing in the 1960s, intensely engaged with his own culture and its complex politics, a novelist like Hugo Claus apparently did not care that his stories would require a special effort on the reader's and above all the translator's part if they were to be understood outside his native Belgium. In sharp contrast, contemporary authors like the Norwegian Per Petterson, the Dutch Gerbrand Bakker, and the Italian Alessandro Baricco offer us works that require no such knowledge or effort, nor the rewards that such effort will bring. More importantly, the language is kept simple. Kazuo Ishiguro has spoken of the importance of avoiding word play and allusion to make things easy for the translator. Scandinavian writers I know tell me they avoid character names that would be difficult for an English reader.

If culture-specific clutter and linguistic virtuosity have become impediments, other strategies are seen positively: the deployment of highly visible tropes immediately recognizable as "literary" and "imaginative," analogous to the wearisome lingua franca of special effects in contemporary cinema, and the foregrounding of a political sensibility that places the author among those "working for world peace." So the overstated fantasy devices of a Rushdie or a Pamuk always go hand in hand with a certain liberal position since, as Borges once remarked, most people have so little aesthetic sense they rely on other criteria to judge the works they read.

What seems doomed to disappear, or at least to risk neglect, is the kind of work that revels in the subtle nuances of its own language and literary culture, the sort of writing that can savage or celebrate the way this or that linguistic group really lives. In the global literary market there will be no place for any Barbara Pyms or Natalia Ginzburgs. Shakespeare would have eased off the puns. A new Jane Austen can forget the Nobel.

READING IT WRONG

HOW FAR IS language really able to communicate something new, something that runs contrary to my expectations? Or rather, how far will I allow it to do so?

One of the intriguing aspects of teaching translation is watching students struggle with sentences that say things they didn't expect them to say. They are used, of course, to the process of passing from not understanding a foreign text to understanding it, that moment when a seemingly meaningless drift of words suddenly falls into place. But they also know that they often make mistakes. They must be careful. If the text says something ordinary and commonplace, there will be little doubt in their minds: "This is the kind of thing people say. It must be OK." But if a writer should come up with some perplexing idea, or, worse still, some declaration running contrary to received wisdom or political correctness, then anxiety sets in; the words will be examined and re-examined even if their individual meaning and the overall syntax is fairly clear. In many cases, especially if the novelty is expressed subtly, students, but also practiced translators, will end up reducing the text to something more conventional.

This tic can take the form of introducing words a translator thinks should be there but aren't. Take this fairly innocuous example: In

D. H. Lawrence's *Women in Love*, Ursula reflects that she's not even tempted to get married. Her sister, Gudrun, agrees and carries on, "Isn't it an amazing thing... how strong the temptation is, not to!" Lawrence comments: "They both laughed, looking at each other. In their hearts they were frightened." A recent Italian edition of the book offers something that, translated back into English, would give, "They both burst out laughing, looking at each other. But deep in their hearts they were afraid."

Experimenting over the years I've realized that if I ask a class of students to translate this into Italian, approximately half will introduce that *but*. It appears to be received wisdom that one doesn't laugh if one is afraid; hence when Lawrence puts the two things together, translators feel a *but* is required to acknowledge the unusualness of this state of affairs. Lawrence on the other hand suggests that nothing is more common than laughing and being afraid; one laughs *because* afraid, in order to deny fear.

However, what is most interesting about this phenomenon is that when I quiz the students, most will admit they were unaware of having introduced the *but*. They actually *read* the text like that. Which means, one can only suppose, that a vast number of ordinary readers will be reading it like that too. Indeed, what I'm suggesting is that the kind of slippage we see in translations is probably indicative of an even greater slippage among many readers who are not of course considering the text as closely as the translator does.

This kind of automatic correction toward what the translator or reader expects can work in all kinds of ways. Later in *Women in Love* Lawrence describes how a sexual experience can induce a state of deep calm. Having made hurried love to Birkin in the back room of an inn, Ursula finds herself in unusually good form pouring the tea. Lawrence heaps on the significance with some unusual usages of the verb *forget* and the adjectives *still* and *perfect*:

She was usually nervous and uncertain at performing these public duties, such as giving tea. But today she forgot, she was at her ease, entirely forgetting to have misgivings. The tea-pot poured beautifully from a proud slender spout. Her eyes were warm with smiles as she gave him his tea. She had learned at last to be still and perfect.

The Italian translator has trouble with this, perhaps finds it embarrassing—in any event, resists. If we translate the Italian version back into English we have Ursula "entirely forgetting that she was inclined to be apprehensive"—a rather more standard statement than "forgetting to have misgivings." But more remarkably, for the last sentence: "Finally she had learned to do it with a firm hand and perfect composure." As if Lawrence had merely been talking about her tea-pouring abilities.

Do we as readers subconsciously make these "corrections"? How far can they go? One of the things that always surprises me when talking about Virginia Woolf's *Mrs. Dalloway* is how little attention is given to the fact that this novel presents the suicide of one of its characters as a gift of individual to collective, on a par with, or at least comparable to, the party that Mrs. Dalloway throws for her well-to-do friends, or indeed the writing of the book itself. These are not fashionable or "safe" thoughts. At the crucial moment, when Septimus Warren Smith, feeling threatened by another doctor's visit, throws himself from the window onto the railings below, he yells, "I'll give it to you!" The Italian translation offers, "*Lo volete voi,*" which in English literally is "It's you who want it!" or, more idiomatically, "You asked for it!" Was the translator aware she had altered the text?

It's true that Septimus is frightened and angry, but the idea of the gift is essential to the book. Do readers, for the main, take the idea on board? To judge by how often this novel is seen as a rather flowery manifestation of soft feminism, I suspect not. Curiously, this Italian translator also has a habit of removing any unpleasantly disparaging comments Woolf makes. When Clarissa Dalloway is described as "a radiancy no doubt in some dull lives," the translation omits the *dull*. In general all that is snobbish in Woolf or Clarissa is gently removed.

Interestingly, exactly the opposite occurs when Machiavelli is rendered into English. Again expectation is everything, and Machiavelli is celebrated of course for being *Machiavellian*. Received opinion must not shift. So when having considered the downfall of his hero and model, the ruthless Cesare Borgia, Machiavelli rather ruefully writes:

> *Raccolte io adunque tutte le azioni del duca, non saprei riprenderlo.*
> (Literally: "Having gathered then all the actions of the duke, I would not know how to reproach him.")

The translator George Bull gives, "So having summed up all that the duke did, I cannot possibly censure him." Here the word *censure* has a strong moral connotation, made stronger still by the introduction of *cannot possibly*, which is not there in the Italian. In line with the author's reputation for cynicism, Bull has Machiavelli insist that he has no *moral* objections to anything Cesare Borgia did. Actually, Machiavelli simply says Borgia didn't make any big mistakes. The true scandal of Machiavelli is that he never considers moral criteria at all—he doesn't feel they are applicable to a politician fighting for survival. But it is easier for us to think of an evil Machiavelli than a lucid thinker deciding that good and evil do not come into it.

In short, there is a tension between reader and text that the translator experiences in a special way because, rewriting the text in his own language, he has to allow that tension to happen again for a new group of readers. Becoming aware of how you might instinctively wish to change a text and eliminate the tension is both to understand the book better and to understand something about yourself.

WHY READERS DISAGREE

"I LOVE THE new DeLillo."

"And I hate it."

It's a familiar conversation: like against dislike with no possible resolution. Or alternatively: "I can't see why *Freedom* upsets you so much. I didn't like it either, but who cares?" Interest against disinterest; as when your wife/brother/friend/colleague raves about some Booker or Pulitzer winner and you feel vaguely guilty. "Sure," you agree, "great writing, intriguing stuff." But the truth is you just couldn't find the energy to finish the book.

So, is there anything we can say about such different responses? Or must we just accept *De gustibus non disputandum est*? The fact is that traditional critical analysis, however brilliant, however much it may help us to understand a novel, rarely alters the color of our initial response. Enthusiasm or disappointment may be confirmed or attenuated, but only exceptionally reversed. We say: James Wood/Colm Tóibín/Michiko Kakutani admires the book and has given convincing reasons for doing so, but I still feel it is the worst kind of crowd-pleaser.

Let me offer a possible explanation that has been developing in my mind over a decade and more. It's a central tenet of systemic psychology that each personality develops in the force field of a community of origin, usually a family, seeking his or her own position in a pre-existing group, or "system," most likely made up of mother, father, brothers and sisters, then aunts, uncles, grandparents, and so on. The leading Italian psychologist, Valeria Ugazio, further suggests that this family "system" also has "semantic content"; that is, as conversations in the family establish criteria for praise and criticism of family members and nonmembers, one particular theme or issue will dominate.

In my family, for example, the quality that mattered most was never courage or independence, success or community spirit, but goodness, usually understood as renunciation. My father was an evangelical clergyman and both parents were involved in the Charismatic Movement. Every person, every political issue, was understood in terms of good and evil. In another family, appraisal might revolve chiefly around, say, the courage and independence someone has shown, or the extent to which another person is timorous and dependent. In such a family it's a fair bet that one member will have shown a remarkable spirit of adventure while another rarely takes risks of any kind.

That is—according to Ugazio's theory—family members tend to manifest the qualities, positive and negative, around which the group's conversations revolve. So it was that at a certain point in his adolescence, my brother made a great show of being "evil" in the terms my parents understood the word: he grew his hair long, drank, smoked dope, locked himself in his room with cute girlfriends, and even told us, with a fair parody of a malignant grin, that he was demonic. As the youngest of three, I found my own adolescence shaped by constant parental pressure to choose between my "bad" brother and "good" sister who played the guitar in church and dressed with exemplary propriety.

Each developing family member, this theory suggests, will be look-ing to find a stable position within the polarized values the family is most concerned with. Persons who for some reason find this difficult, perhaps drawn emotionally one way and intellectually another, might eventually develop symptoms of psychological unease; they cannot figure out where they stand in the group; which, in a family, might not be far from saying that they don't quite know who they are.

In her remarkable book *Semantic Polarities and Psychopathologies in the Family: Permitted and Forbidden Stories* (2013), Ugazio offers examples of this process from celebrated novels: all members of the Karamazov family, she points out, can be understood by placing them on the good-evil axis: the wicked Dimitri, the saintly Alyosha, and the more complex and untrustworthy Ivan who oscillates be-tween the extremes. In *Tess of the D'Urbervilles*, on the other hand, the characters are fearful or reckless, patient or courageous, pusil-lanimous or bold. Of course they have other qualities too; they are complex, fully-drawn people, but it is their position along the fear-courage axis that is decisive as the plot unfolds. Moral issues in Thomas Hardy's work usually present themselves in the form: Do I have the courage/recklessness to break this conventional moral rule?

When writing reviews I have occasionally used this kind of ap-proach to help me get a fix on a writer. Reading through scores of Chekhov's stories recently, I became aware that the key issue through-out was belonging: Do I belong, the characters ask themselves, to this family/institution/social class, or don't I? Am I excluded from this relationship, am I merely trapped in this marriage? Most of the cen-tral characters display an ambivalence about whether they want to be part of the group or not: or rather, they want to be part, but then feel diminished by this belonging. They need to feel superior to the group or relationship as well as being in it; they need to escape, but if they do, they are immediately anxious to return.

So far so good. But let's take the argument a little further than Ugazio does. Systemic theorists (or "positioning theorists" as more recent jargon would have it) see people as constantly taking the position developed within the family out into the larger world. Some of them go so far as to say that identity is no more (no less!) than the position one consistently adopts, or seeks to adopt, in each new situation. As a result, misunderstandings may occur—at work perhaps, or in a newly formed couple—between people who have grown up with quite different criteria for assessing behavior and establishing a position in relation to it. Hence expressions like: "I don't know where she's coming from"; "He really doesn't get it, does he?"

Could not something of the same failure of two psyches to mesh occur between writers and readers? Or alternatively, might not the psyches of writer and reader mesh all too powerfully, but in quarrel rather than harmony?

For example, not only does a writer like Chekhov focus constantly on issues of belonging and escape, but he does so in such a way as to invite our sympathy for the complex behavioral strategy that he personally always adopted: an attitude of generous involvement with others that nevertheless safeguards absolute independence and allows him to retain a certain separateness and superiority. Many of Chekhov's stories, about people trapped in relationships on the one hand, or excluded from their peer groups on the other, might be read as warnings to himself (the author) not to change this strategy. Not all readers will connect with this.

Or we might consider D. H. Lawrence. In *Sons and Lovers* the moral veto that Miriam places on sex before marriage is "unmasked" by her boyfriend, Paul, as merely fear finding an alibi in moral convention. In an extremely bold move Paul declares fear to be the evil, not sex. Victorian morality is turned on its head; for those in love, Paul insists, making love is a *moral* imperative. Fear is a betrayal of life.

While writing this novel, Lawrence ran off with a married woman, encouraging her to abandon her husband and three young children. Reading Lawrence's strange *Study of Thomas Hardy*, we can see that he was intensely locked into Hardy's imaginative world; the two of them shared the same need to find a position on issues of fear (one thinks of a poem like Lawrence's "Snake"). But what he hated in Hardy was that his characters so often choose not to be courageous, or when they are bold and defy convention the gesture is presented as merely reckless and they are destroyed by it. He must always "stand with the average against the exception," Lawrence complains.

It's interesting that in his time Hardy's novels were severely criticized for being immoral, because they suggested that society's crushing of sinners and above all adulterers was cruel. Today there is no such criticism and we all (excluding, perhaps, evangelicals like my parents) side gladly with Tess, Jude, and Hardy's many other victims of Victorian severity. We have a different take on life and on Hardy's novels because we grew up in different systems. Lawrence, on the other hand, has enjoyed no such turnaround in reader response. He is so forthright as a storyteller, so determined to have his way, and so blithely unconcerned when a pusillanimous character is brushed aside by anyone who has the courage to live life to the full; one thinks of poor Banford in *The Fox*, dispatched without pity because she stands in the way of Henry and March's marriage, or indeed of Professor Weekley himself, whom Lawrence deprived of an extraordinary wife.

What I'm suggesting then is that much of our response to novels may have to do with the kind of "system" or "conversation" we grew up in and within which we had to find a position and establish an identity. Dostoevsky is always and immediately enthralling for me. The question of whether and how far to side with good or evil, with renunciation or indulgence, grabs me at once and takes me straight back to my adolescence. And how I loathe the end of his books where the sinner repents and gets on his knees and sees the error of his ways in an ecstasy of self-abasement. I love Dostoevsky, but I argue furiously with him. Same with an author like Coetzee in *Disgrace*. I feel locked into argument with him. Beyond any question of "liking" these books are important to me.

On the other hand, when I read the Norwegian writer Per Petterson, who again is chiefly concerned with fear—vulnerability to the elements and the terror of being abandoned by those we have most trusted—I immensely admire his writing, but find it hard to care. When asked on two occasions to review Petterson, I read every word carefully and with pleasure and gave the novels the praise they very much deserve, but I wouldn't go out of my way to read another book of his. His world, the disturbing imagery he draws on, the rhythm and pacing of his sentences, are far removed from my concerns. Affinities, as Goethe tells us, are important. Few works of art can have universal appeal.

WHERE I'M READING FROM

IT'S NOW A commonplace that there is no "correct" reading of any book: we all find something different in a novel. Yet little is said of particular readers and particular readings, and critics continue to offer interpretations they hope will be authoritative, even definitive. In this regard, I've been thinking how useful it might be if all of us "professionals" were to put on record—some dedicated website perhaps—a brief account of how we came to hold the views we do on books, or at least how we *think* we came to hold them. If each of us stated where we were coming from, perhaps some light could be thrown on our disagreements. Here is my own contribution.

Books began, in my case, when my parents read to me, so I knew from the start that reading must be a "good" thing. Fervently evangelical—a clergyman and his wife—my parents only did things that were good. They read us children's stories and the Bible. Later I exploited this faith of theirs in the essential goodness of literature to plot my escape from the suffocating world in which they lived and wanted everyone else to live.

When they read to us, a daughter and two sons, perhaps beside a smoldering coal fire, with an evening cup of cocoa, the books created a feeling of togetherness; we were united in one place in the thrall of one parental voice, my mother's usually, and afterward there was a shared store of stories and memories that made us a family. But when I read alone, searching out books that offered a broader view of life, books isolated me and divided us. Now I had ideas and arguments that countered theirs. I read avidly, safe in the knowledge that they thought this was a good thing. But soon enough they picked up my copy of Gide, of Beckett, of Nietzsche; then there were tears and conflict. Away from the Bible and children's books, reading was *not* always good, and when it wasn't good it was bad. Very bad.

Even today there is a subtle tension in my reading between the desire to free myself from the immediate community with its received ideas, and the desire to share what I read with those around me, those I love. On the other hand, it was perfectly clear to me in adolescence that when we read alone, each member of the family would choose quite different books, and that what you were reading inevitably declared where you stood on the things that mattered in our house. You had to be careful when you chose to share a book.

My father's study was wall-to-wall Bible concordances, huge tomes in scab-red covers, each brittle page divided into two yellowing columns and dustily flecked with text references, brackets, footnotes. A glance was enough to tell me I would never read them. Perhaps they inspired my lifelong impatience with books that seem overtechnical: jargon-ridden works of literary criticism, for example. I connect them with my father. There was something unhappily withdrawn about his study; he hated noise; no one could challenge him in his knowledge of the scriptures. But it did not seem like all that cross-referencing had much to do with living and breathing. My family created a situation where I went to books for fresh air, not scholarship.

Mother had no shelves of her own but supplied the books kept in a small rotating mahogany bookcase in the living room; these were family books where goodness was not a theory or theology but a question of warm, benevolent emotions or, perhaps, swashbuckling patriotism. Dickens had the most space I suppose, closely followed by the adventure stories of a British World War II pilot with the improbable name of Captain Bigglesworth. John Buchan was there, and *The Secret Garden*, and *Water Babies*, and of course, *Three Men in a Boat*. This was permitted reading. I read them all and felt hungrier than ever.

Right at the back of the cubbyhole under the stairs, where you had to get on your knees as the ceiling came down to meet the floor, wrapped in thick brown paper and tied in string, was a book published in the 1940s about marriage and sex; it included some instructions as to how to go about making love if you never had before. Things like: Don't be in a hurry to get all your clothes off. Think of your partner's pleasure as much as your own. This book, whose title I have forgotten, was hugely useful to me. It was also interesting to discover that my righteous parents did this stuff, and again that the book could not appear on other shelves in the house. Evidently, there were books that were good, or for the good, but not good for everyone at every moment.

In my sister's room, painted pink with flowery curtains and a pink bedspread, the shelves were full of Georgette Heyer and similar romances of a historical flavor. At some point I must have noticed the relationship between the book covers and the room's decor. This was the aura my sister moved in. Five years older than me, she played the guitar in church and was always prayerful; anything to do with sex had to come in a patina of propriety and pink. I read about half of a Georgette Heyer novel, but did not find it useful.

My brother, the middle child, was the rebel. In his bookshelf, among sundry science fiction by Asimov and Ballard, not even hidden, was a paperback called *Lasso Round the Moon* by Agnar Mykle, published in 1954 (the year I was born). Paperbacks were new to me.

There was a photograph on the cover that promised sensual not spiritual bliss. I understood at once that only certain sections of this volume need be read. They were already well thumbed.

It will seem all too easy, this fusion of topography and attitude, but it's true: my room was sandwiched between my brother's and my sister's. It too had a bookshelf. There were no rosy historical romances, no girls clutching a last shred of clothing to their modesty. There were no concordances, no innocent children's books. Way before I could possibly understand them, there were Tolstoy and Dostoevsky and Chekhov and Flaubert and Zola. These books were foreign. Out of it. They never gave me the crasser joys I craved, but then again they never made me feel I was merely indulging, or merely provoking; I wasn't locked in a fight with my parents, as it seemed to me my brother was. Neither good nor bad, they were good *and* bad, there was adventure and debate. If my parents made the whole world black and white, these books were colored and immensely complicated.

Over the past year or two I've realized how much this organization of the books in my childhood home still influences my reading and reviewing. When I negatively reviewed a book like William Giraldi's *Busy Monsters*, it was because it seemed to me an exercise in literary exhibitionism; intellectuality as an end in itself, self-indulgent performance whose main intention was to encourage the reader to concede that the author was smart, rather as if those biblical concordances had been rewritten by Agnar Mykle. When I admired aspects of Dave Eggers it was because I recognized his constant division of the world into good and evil, and when I doubted him it was because in the end it seemed to me he was preaching. The analyses I offered of *Fifty Shades of Grey* and Stieg Larsson's *Millennium* trilogy were very much operations in understanding their position in the geography of our old family bookshelves. Funnily enough, their immense success immediately makes sense when described in this way.

They are both books that allow you to read a little hard violent sex while siding with a hero or heroine eager to eliminate such things from the world. Anyone turning to my piece on Peter Matthiessen in *The New York Review of Books* will now understand both my attraction to his novel *In Paradise* and my reservations.

Will I never escape from this? Is it a miserable limitation? Should they stop commissioning reviews from me? We all have our positions. Identity is largely a question of the pattern of our responses when presented with a new situation, a new book. Certainly the idea of impartiality is a chimera. To be impartial about narrative would be to come from nowhere, to be no one.

The challenge, I suppose, is to be aware of one's habits, to be ready to negotiate, even to surprise oneself. Perhaps it's the books that very slightly shift an old position, or at least oblige you to think it through again, that become most precious. I still recall my perplexity, then growing pleasure, when I read Peter Stamm a couple of years ago: first a sense that his novels were truly different; not the fireworks of would-be experimentalism, but a voice I hadn't heard before. I had to struggle to place it, to find where I stood in relation to it. Essentially, Stamm constructs stories that my background leads me to think of as moral dilemmas—as in the case of a long extramarital affair in which the mistress falls pregnant—but that his characters understand entirely in terms of fear and courage, dependence and independence. The writing is, if I can put it this way, comically serious, in its simultaneous awareness of and refusal to engage with the moral side of events. In the end I was fascinated.

II
The Book in the World

WHAT'S WRONG WITH THE NOBEL?

SO THE SWEDISH poet Tomas Tranströmer wins the Nobel Prize. Aside from a couple of long poems available on the Internet, I haven't read Tranströmer, yet I feel sure this is a good decision in every way. Above all for the Nobel jury. Let me explain.

There are eighteen of them, members of an organization called the Swedish Academy, which back at the end of the nineteenth century was given the task of awarding the Nobel. At the time two members suggested it was a mistake to accept the job. The Academy's founding brief, back in 1786, was to promote the "purity, strength, and sublimity of the Swedish language." Was this compatible with choosing the finest oeuvre of "an idealistic tendency" from anywhere in the world?

All members of the Academy are Swedish and most of them hold full time professorial jobs in Swedish universities. On the present jury there are just five women, and no woman has ever held the presidency. Only one member was born after 1960. This is partly because you cannot resign from the Academy. It's a life sentence. So there's rarely any new blood. For the past few years, however, two members have refused to cooperate with deliberations for the prize because of previous disagreements, one over the reaction, or lack of it, to the fatwa against Salman Rushdie and the other over awarding the prize to Elfriede Jelinek, a writer whom the dissenting member felt was "chaotic and pornographic."

How do these people decide who are the greatest novelists and/or poets of the day on the international scene? They call on scores of literary experts in scores of countries and pay them to put down a few reflections about possible winners. Such experts are supposed to remain anonymous, but inevitably some have turned out to be acquaintances of those they have nominated.

Let's try to imagine how much reading is involved. Assume that a hundred writers are nominated every year—it's not unthinkable—and that the jury starts by reading one book from each of them. But of course this is a prize that goes to the whole oeuvre of a writer, so let's suppose that as they hone down the number of candidates they now read two books of those who remain, then three, then four. It's not unlikely that each year they are faced with reading two hundred books (this on top of their ordinary workloads). Of these books, very few will be written in Swedish and only some will be available in Swedish translation; many will be in English, or available in English translation. But since the English and Americans notoriously don't translate a great deal, some reading will have to be done in French, German, or perhaps Spanish translations from more exotic originals.

Remember that we're talking about poems as well as novels and that these works are coming from all over the world, many intensely engaged with cultures and literary traditions of which the members of the Swedish Academy understandably and forgivably know little. So it's a heterogeneous and taxing bunch of books these professors have to digest and compare, every year. Responding recently to criticism that in the last ten years seven prizes have gone to Europeans, Peter Englund, the president of the current jury, claimed its members were well equipped for English but concerned about their strengths in such languages as Indonesian. Fair enough.

Let's pause for a moment, here, and imagine our Swedish professors, called to uphold the purity of the Swedish language, as they compare a poet from Indonesia, perhaps translated into English, a novelist from Cameroon, perhaps available only in French, and another who writes in Afrikaans but is published in German and Dutch, and then a towering celebrity like Philip Roth, who they could of course read in English, but might equally feel tempted, if only out of a sense of exhaustion, to look at in Swedish.

Do we envy them this task? Does it make much sense? The two members who a century ago felt the cup should be allowed to pass from them were worried that the Academy would become "a cosmopolitan tribunal of literature." Something they instinctively felt was problematic. They were not wrong.

Now, let's imagine that we have been condemned for life to making, year in year out a burdensome and nearly impossible decision to which the world increasingly and inexplicably ascribes a crazy importance. How do we go about it? We look for some simple, rapid, and broadly acceptable criteria that will help us get this pain out of the way. And since, as Borges himself noted, aesthetics are difficult and require a special sensibility and long reflection while political affiliations are easier and quickly grasped, we begin to identify those areas of the world that have grabbed public attention, perhaps because of political turmoil or abuses of human rights; we find those authors who have already won a huge level of respect and possibly major prizes in the literary communities of these countries and who are outspokenly committed to the right side of whatever political divide we're talking about, and we select them.

So we have the period when the Nobel went to Eastern-bloc

dissidents, or to South American writers against dictatorship, or South African writers against apartheid, or, most amazingly, to the anti-Berlusconi playwright Dario Fo, whose victory caused some bewilderment in Italy. It was an honorable enough formula but alas not every trouble spot (Tibet, Chechnya) boasts its great dissident writer, to which we might add that since the prize is perceived as going to the country as much as to the writer, it's not possible to give it to writers from the same trouble spot two years running. What a conundrum!

Sometimes the jurists clearly get their fingers burned. Having received so many major literary prizes in Germany and Austria, the left-wing feminist Jelinek seemed a safe choice in 2004. But her work is ferocious, often quite indigestible (she'd never win a literary prize in, say, Italy or England), and the novel *Greed*, in particular, which appeared shortly before her Nobel was awarded, was truly unreadable. I know because I tried, and tried again. Had the members of the jury really read it? You have to wonder. Not surprisingly, after the controversy caused by Jelinek's victory, the jury fell back on obvious choices for a couple of years: Pinter, politically appropriate and half forgotten; then Vargas Llosa, whom I somehow imagined had already won the prize many years before.

What a relief then from time to time to say, the hell with it and give it to a Swede, in this case the octogenarian acknowledged as his nation's finest living poet and a man whose whole oeuvre, as Peter Englund charmingly remarks, could fit into a single slim paperback. A winner, in short, whom the whole jury can read in the original pure Swedish in just a few hours. Perhaps they needed a sabbatical. Not to mention the detail, not irrelevant in these times of crisis, that the $1.5-million-dollar prize will stay in Sweden.

But most healthy of all, a decision like this, which we all understand would never have been taken by say, an American jury, or a Nigerian jury, or perhaps above all a Norwegian jury, reminds us of the essential silliness of the prize and our own foolishness at taking it seriously. Eighteen (or sixteen) Swedish nationals will have a certain credibility when weighing up works of Swedish literature—so we can feel assured that Tranströmer really is an excellent poet—but what group could ever really get its mind round the infinitely varied work of scores of different traditions? And why should we ask them to do that?

A GAME WITHOUT RULES

IN 1904, THREE years after the first Nobel Prize in Literature was awarded to the French poet Sully Prudhomme, the English Football Association chose not to participate in the formation of an International Football Federation (FIFA). Members could not see the point. Nor, in 1930, the year in which Sinclair Lewis won the Nobel, did the English participate in the first World Cup: they objected to the prospect of a ten-day ocean crossing to Uruguay to play teams that meant nothing to them. The first international football game, they pointed out, had been between England and Scotland, in 1872—a time when Alfred Nobel was still focused on improving his dynamite. Who needs Argentina or Brazil when you have Scotland to play?

I am not the first to draw attention to parallel processes of internationalization in sports and literature. As with many analogies, it is the combination of similarity and difference that is illuminating. For all the different styles of play in different countries and continents, football is a game whose rules can be universally applied. North Korea plays Mexico with a Swedish referee and despite one or two contested offside decisions a result is recorded and one team can pass to the next round without too much discussion. But can we feel so certain when the Swedish referee judges poems from those two countries that he will pick the right winner? Or even that there is a "right" winner? Or even a competition? The Mexican did not write his or her poems with the idea of getting a winning decision over the North Korean, or with a Swedish referee in mind. At least we hope not.

The interesting thing, then, about the English refusal to participate in the early World Cups is that, although there was no real obstacle to measuring themselves against teams from far away, they did not feel that this competition for notional world supremacy was what the sport was *for*. What mattered was familiar communities confronting each other in the stadium—that would give meaning to the game.

Vice versa, what is fascinating about international literary prizes is that the obstacles to choosing between writers coming from different cultures and working in different languages are so evident and daunting as to render the task almost futile; yet such is the appetite for international prizes and for winners that people do everything possible to overlook this. So what is the underlying purpose of these prizes? To what extent are novelists—like athletes in the Olympics, or soccer players in the World Cup—being asked to contribute to the building of a vast and for the moment largely imaginary global culture? In what way does this change the kind of literature that gets written, and the way it is written and talked about?

These questions were the subject of a conference on global literature that I and my colleague, the Milanese poet Edoardo Zuccato, organized at IULM University in Milan in 2012. In the opening presentation, David Damrosch, head of comparative literature at Harvard and founder of the World Institute for Literature, rather unexpectedly focused on the work of Rudyard Kipling. Based in Lahore, the twenty-year-old Kipling had started out writing for the local Anglo-Indian community, publishing his short stories in the city's newspaper. Later, as he became aware of a wider readership in England and the United States, he developed all kinds of strategies for making his fiction more accessible to readers who would know little of India; gradually, Damrosch suggested, discovering and "explaining" India became a central part of Kipling's work.

Thus begins the development of a kind of literary fiction that is largely detached from debates internal to a nation and presented instead as an opportunity to discover a distant community and a sense of our place in a larger world. One important stop along this road was the explosion of South American magical realism, which enjoyed its defining moment with Gabriel García Márquez's *One Hundred Years of Solitude.* In the work of Márquez, Carlos Fuentes, Isabel Allende, Julio Cortázar, Mario Vargas Llosa, and others, magical realism offered Americans and Europeans an account of South America in which it was honestly hard to see much difference in spirit or atmosphere between the dozens of countries and communities of this vast continent.

The Mexican novelist Jorge Volpi, who is very much in favor of internationalization, nevertheless points out how difficult it had become at the height of magical realism for South American writers to get themselves published if they didn't subscribe to this highly stylized vision of literature. At the conference he explained how in the 1990s a group of Chilean writers formed the so-called McOndo group (an ironic reformulation of Macondo, the central location in *One Hundred Years of Solitude*), complaining that by gaining the approval of powerful readerships abroad, magical realism was preventing South American writers from recounting the more prosaic truths about the continent.

Magical realism was not, of course, confined to South America. Among others, a number of Anglo-Indian authors used their own versions of the style to create a new vision of India for international readers; one of those authors was so spectacularly out of touch with the nation he was supposedly presenting to the West that the violent reaction to his *Satanic Verses* after its publication in India caught him entirely by surprise. Francesca Orsini, a scholar of Hindi literature (and an Italian academic working at the University of London), posed an interesting question: There are many important books written in the languages of the subcontinent and then translated into English, among them Bhalchandra Nemade's *Cocoon*, Vinod Kumar Shukla's *The Servant's Shirt*, Geetanjali Shree's *Mai*, and Krishna Sobti's *The Heart Has Its Reasons*. Why do they not have the same international success as works by Anglo-Indian authors like Rushdie, Vikram Seth, and Arundhati Roy? Translation, she remarked, could make a novel available, but the real exoticism of the truly foreign text remained a barrier to most readers.

Zuccato, the Milanese poet, might have been answering her when he made an impassioned attack on the whole concept of postcolonial literature. He suggested that those postwar writers in Africa and India who had chosen to write in English and French for the international community have not only given us a superficial and easily consumed exoticism; in doing so they have made it less likely that a Western public will make the effort to read those working in the local languages and offering something that would be genuinely "other" from the Western novel package we are used to. The Milan-based literary agent Marco Vigevani rather confirmed this when he pointed out the situation of Arab-language writers such as the Lebanese Hassan Daoud and the Egyptian Makkawi Said, who work in traditional genres that mix poetry and prose and that have no Western corollary. Prominent in the Arab world, these writers get almost no attention in the West because nobody has any idea how to read the kind of works they write even when they are translated.

What I found fascinating, as this discussion bounced back and forth, was that no one seemed to accept the idea that it might be enough to address one's own community, that perhaps it was not strictly necessary to appear in this global space or contribute to its formation. Why should the literary world allow itself to be hijacked by this larger project?

The ideal of a single world community is an entirely honorable thing, but when literature (like football) becomes an instrument for creating that community, then there are other implications that may not be so attractive. Bas Heijne, a Dutch essayist and critic, suggested that globalization invites us to see our own cultures as foreign and minor and even proposed that as English dominates the international literary scene, fiction is becoming more and more self-referential and less genuinely engaged with any society. However, despite Heijne's fascinating arguments, none of his own considerable body of work is available in English. Who would translate a Dutch essayist? According to one ominous prediction, fielded in David Crystal's book *Language Death*, by 2100 between 50 and 90 percent of the world's languages will have disappeared.

Was the IULM conference itself part of this process? With speakers from many countries, all the sessions and discussions were in English. Some later complained that the novelists who participated, and who do not write in English, Peter Stamm and Jorge Volpi, should have read at least something in their native languages and not exclusively in English translation, though the writers themselves seemed happy enough to read in the language most widely understood. Some of the English participants found the accents of those speaking English as a second language hard to handle. Some of the nonacademics found the academic jargon of one or two high-powered professors incomprehensible, even though they shared the same tongue, while an Italian doctorate student told me she found the academics easier to understand, because Italians are all too used to scholarly jargon; it was the colloquialisms and accents of the non-academic, native English speakers she found impossible.

Yet curiously, despite all this trouble communicating, everybody seemed happy simply to be there. Sometimes, perhaps, it's not important really to understand, but simply to feel one is present and participating in the huge new community that is forming.

MOST FAVORED NATIONS

SHORTLY BEFORE HIS death in 1980, the great anthropologist Gregory Bateson suggested that social engineering was like trying to reverse a truck with five or six trailers attached to it through a complex maze; you might get somewhere, but where and with what collateral damage would never be clear. So it's hardly a surprise that the decision in many countries around Europe to insist on English as a second language—to facilitate trade of course and to promote a global scientific community—has had some unexpected effects, not least on literature.

In Milan, where I live, the city polytechnic has announced that some graduate programs are soon to be taught exclusively in English. But Italy is hardly in the forefront. About 56 percent of Europeans speak a second language, and for 38 percent of them that language is English. In Scandinavia and the Netherlands, where it's fairly common to find university courses taught in English, the figure is more like 90 percent. Even where the percentage is smaller we are nevertheless talking about the most educated part of the community, those more likely to be reading novels, particularly literary novels.

Inevitably, as the number of people speaking English increases, so do the sales of novels in English. But not enormously. The surprise is that increased knowledge of English has also brought a much more marked increase in sales of literature written in English but read in translation in the local language. When you learn a language you don't just pick up a means of communication, you buy into a culture, you get interested.

Statistics provided by the Dutch Fund for Literature show that while the number of Dutch translations of works coming from other languages has been static, or risen only slowly, as English is taught more and more widely in schools and universities there has been a huge leap in translations from English. In 1946 only 5 percent of Holland's book production was made up of translations; by 2005 it had reached 35 percent, and in the area of prose fiction the share had grown to 71 percent. Of those translations, 75 percent now come from English. What figures I have managed to find for Germany and Italy do not differ a great deal.

At IULM University in Milan, we have a group research project on the effects of globalization on literature. Last year, as part of this project, I went to Holland, where publishers and readers have always been generous to me, and over a month spent a number of afternoons in a bookshop in the center of Amsterdam talking to customers about their reading choices. All in all I managed forty fifteen-minute interviews with "ordinary" readers aged between twenty and sixty and evenly distributed between men and women; all but one older interviewee told me they read mainly foreign novels.

When I asked people to list titles they had recently read, they seemed surprised themselves how prevalently English and American, rather than simply foreign, these novels were. A linguist from Amsterdam University, for example, went away and jotted down the names of all the novelists on his shelves: fifty-eight Anglophone authors (many were Booker and Pulitzer winners), nineteen from eight other countries and twenty Dutch. Until he wrote down this list, he remarked, he had not been aware how far his reading was driven by publicity and availability. Indeed, no one spoke of any method behind his or her choice of novels (as opposed to nonfiction, where people declared very specific and usually local interests).

"I read foreign novels because they're better," was a remark I began to expect. (Surprisingly, a senior member of the Dutch Fund for Literature also said this to me.) I asked readers if that could really be the case; why would foreign books be "better" across the board, in what way? As the responses mounted up, a pattern emerged: these people had learned excellent English and with it an interest in Anglo-Saxon culture in their school years. They had come to use their novel reading (but not other kinds of reading) to reinforce this alternative identity, a sort of parallel or second life that complemented the Dutch reality they lived in and afforded them a certain self-esteem as initiates in a wider world.

Apart from the immediate repercussions on the book market, where there is now fierce competition between English and Dutch editions of English-language novels, the phenomenon suggests a few things about reading and the modern psyche. There appears to be a tension, or perhaps necessary balance, between evasion and realism in fiction, between the desire to read seriously about real things—to feel that one is not wasting time, but engaging intelligently with the world—and simultaneously the desire to escape the confines of one's immediate community, move into the territory of the imagination, and perhaps fantasize about faraway places.

For Europeans, one way to satisfy both desires is to read novels translated from English. These works tend to talk about a culture that is to them far away but relevant because of the dominance of Anglo-Saxon and specifically American culture worldwide, and because they themselves have acquired English as a second language; in most translations there will usually be some memory or trace of the original language, which, for those who are familiar with it, will reinforce their sense of knowing that other world. This may be simply the names of people or places, references to customs or a cultural setting, or, inevitably, some syntactical or lexical habit that appears more often in, say, translations from English than in normal local language use (the frequency of the present progressive is a typical marker).

The Dutch readers I interviewed told me they only really noticed that a text was translated, rather than originally written in Dutch, when the translation had been made from a language they knew. Then they could occasionally hear the English or French or German behind the Dutch. But rather than feeling persuaded as a result to give up on translations and tackle their novels in the original language, they seemed to take pleasure in criticizing the translator for having allowed this to happen: a number of interviewees were convinced they could do better themselves, which of course is an encouraging thing to think. Again, the reading experience reinforces self-regard.

Naturally, the more one reads books by English and American authors, and watches movies and soaps made in America and costume dramas made in England, and is exposed to interminable news stories about American primaries and presidential elections, in which Europeans now feel they are somehow participating, the more full and complex this second life becomes and the more pleasure there is in reinforcing it with yet another English or American novel.

Four of my interviewees, however, all in their early twenties, added another reason for choosing English-language novels in translation over Dutch ones, a reason that again had nothing to do with the quality of the books. "You have to read things that you can talk about when you travel," one young woman explained. "Nobody outside Holland knows Dutch novels. It's good to know the big book of the moment, Franzen, Rushdie, what everybody's talking about." It was important to her, she said, when reading a novel, to think that it was being read by people like herself worldwide; it made her feel part of an international community. At moments of travel or contact with foreigners the second life becomes real.

Naturally, authors writing in English benefit enormously from this, yet are usually complacently unaware of their good fortune. Sitting on a panel of British writers at a conference in Berlin last year, I was embarrassed when one of my colleagues, a man known for his fierce left-wing satires of presumptuous public figures, said that the British could feel proud of producing a literature of such quality that all the world wished to read it. Well, it is true that Britain has a strong tradition in novel writing, but these days the dice are so heavily loaded in favor of English-language novels that the question of quality is almost a moot point. In any power game, it seems, the dominant party is the least likely to be aware of what is going on.

These reflections were confirmed when I was among a group of British authors invited to give talks and readings at a charming literary festival—Le Comédie du Livre—in Montpellier. Aside from our formal events, we were asked to sit for a couple of hours a day in open-air bookstalls signing our novels for French readers. It was another opportunity to talk to people about their reading choices.

Now, the French don't speak English as well as the Dutch or Germans, but again, when questioned, almost all of those buying English fiction in French translation said they spoke some English and in general preferred reading foreign/English-language novels to French ones. It's uncanny. And again when I discussed this with my fellow British authors, the idea that their work was being bought for reasons other than content, reputation, and quality came as a surprise and possibly an insult; their second languages are rarely strong and their reading is not guided by identification with another culture.

So, to return to Bateson's unforeseen consequences, partly thanks to the huge increase in English teaching, which is itself in line with the pressures toward globalization, we have a situation where literary fiction is coming to serve a different purpose and to be experienced differently in the different national communities. The politically engaged social novel many European writers (Moravia, Calvino, Sartre, Camus, Böll) were celebrated for writing up to about the 1970s continues in the Anglo-Saxon world, but is fast disappearing in many European countries for the simple reason that people are reading and now perhaps writing rather less about their own societies, and hence novels are less likely to take on national issues. Globalization, it seems, does not homogenize across the board; it may push literature to develop in one way on one side of the Atlantic—or rather the language divide—and in quite a different way on the other.

WRITING ADRIFT IN THE WORLD

EVERY YEAR I send a number of my translation students in Milan to England on an exchange. Years ago they would take general courses in English and American literature; then it was postcolonial literature; now they study "world literature." Looking at the reading lists, which range far and wide chronologically and geographically, from the *Epic of Gilgamesh* to Ernest Hemingway, the *Tale of Genji* to Jorge Luis Borges, it is hard to imagine how a strong sense of the social and cultural settings in which they were produced can be built up around any of the individual works. Or rather, the only relevant context is the human race, planet Earth, post 5000 BCE, circa. The stress will be on the essential and universal rather than the local and accidental; the subtext, as David Shields insists, quoting Montaigne, in a recent polemic on contemporary fiction in *Little Star*, that "Every man contains within himself the entire human condition."

But does he? Or she?

As my part of the deal in this exchange, I tutor students from England studying, or practicing, creative writing. They too now move in an international world, as their coming to Italy to work with me testifies. They too have taken courses in world literature, or at least postcolonial literature. They are familiar with the big international names—Kundera, Pamuk, Eco, Vargas Llosa, Roth, Murakami. They know who won the Nobel, the Man Booker International Prize, the IMPAC, the Pulitzer. Exciting as it is, none of this reading is particularly useful to them. Pamuk, for example, may offer a strong sense of place, but it is one increasingly addressed to those outside Turkey, rather than to the Turkish themselves; is the young English writer to talk about England to a foreign audience? Roth, in contrast, deeply engaged in the American experience, invites the young writer into the now ubiquitous second life that most citizens of the world have as passive observers of American culture, a world that often has little or nothing to do with daily experience elsewhere. In Europe today, one reads less and less about the immediate society one lives in. Assisting young writers as they struggle to find a voice that feels like their own, a style that might imbue what they write with a sense of necessity and urgency, I am reminded of what a literary canon is, or was, and what purpose it served.

For most of us, the set of behaviors we call personality or self forms initially in a family of three, four, or five individuals, then develops as it is exposed to the larger worlds of school and, in our teens perhaps, our town, our country. The richness of our individual personalities is a measure of the complexity of the relations that sustain us. A word spoken at home or school can be dense with nuance and shared knowledge in a way unlikely to occur in a casual exchange at rail station or airport, however fascinating and attractive an exotic traveling companion may be. This is not an argument for staying home, but for having a home from which to set out.

One of the functions of a canon or a national tradition has been to provide a familiar group of texts, stretching from past to present, constitutive of one's own community and within which a writer could establish his position, signaling his similarity and difference from authors around and before him. Nuance is more telling than absolute novelty; the more the similarities, the more what difference there is will count. Hence, it might be more useful for a young English writer to be building up a knowledge of, say, Evelyn Waugh, Elizabeth Bowen, Anthony Powell, Barbara Pym, along with the writers they drew on and the later generation they inspired, than to be mixing Chinua Achebe with Primo Levi. This is not of course a reflection on the stature of these writers—it's simply an observation that many of my students have read so disparately that they have little awareness of a body of texts tackling their own culture and within which they can place their writing.

It is not true, as many will claim, that students of creative writing all produce similar and similarly insipid texts. That is not my experience at all. However, with all the variety, two broad tendencies are evident; let me give extreme examples. One student of mine is writing a historical literary thriller set in the Mongol Empire of the thirteenth century. He is talented, he does his research; he knows how to establish a narrative rhythm, mix dialogue and description, keep the ball rolling and the suspense tightening. Still, it is only when he writes about the warrior hero's being intimidated by his wife and attracted to his dead son's widow that I suddenly feel that something really interesting is beginning to happen, something that matters to the author. This tormented little subplot clearly exists apart from any ambition or research that has gone into planning the book and might have formed the core of a different kind of novel, of which the English tradition offers a variety of models. But in my student's narrative it risks derailing the larger locomotive of the saga. The student drops it and sticks to plan, describing great acts of hubris and colorful battles. I feel fairly sure he will find a publisher.

At the opposite extreme, another student tries to write about what it is like being part of a particular family and group of friends in a specific place in England now. He has a plot: the young hero has contracted HIV in a casual and drunken betrayal of the woman who seemed destined to become his wife. The novel charts the realignment of a web of relationships as the hero and those close to him very slowly learn to accept and deal with his changed reality. The highly specific habits of speech among friends and family are crucial in establishing the community, its vitality and resistance to change. A shift in the way two people address each other takes on great significance and poignancy. As a result, the book, if it's ever published, will make more sense to readers who recognize these speech habits and feel at home with them. The difficulty for this young writer is that despite an excellent ear and fine memory for the idiosyncrasies of speech, he isn't aware of a range of possible models that might help him structure this material and pace it well. I spend much of my time with him suggesting books and plays, old and new, and mostly English, which attempt similar representations and dramas.

In David Shields's polemic against the traditional novel, or rather against those who continue to write it when he believes it has lost its validity, he frequently draws our attention to the fragmented character and accelerated speed of modern life, and the prominence of new media—particularly blogs, Facebook, and other social media. He links this to a general preference for what is both immediately contemporary and "true" or at least "documentary," over traditional fiction. "The key thing for an intellectually rigorous writer to come to grips with," he tells us, "is the marginalization of literature by more technologically sophisticated and thus more visceral forms."

I find it hard to understand why the technologically sophisticated is necessarily more visceral. The viscera are visceral, the old primitive gut: this pain, this pleasure, now. At the same time, I share Shields's weariness with novels that, however elegant and intelligent, appear merely to be going through the motions, to be aimed above all at creating the package that will lead to prominence on the world stage, or at least commercial success (the two are almost the same thing).

If there is a problem with the novel, and I'm agreed with Shields that there is, it is not that it doesn't participate in modern technology, can't talk about it or isn't involved with it; I can download in seconds on my Kindle a novel made up entirely of emails or text messages. Perhaps the problem is rather a slow weakening of the sense of being inside a society with related and competing visions of the world to which writers make their own urgent narrative contributions; this being replaced by authors who take courses to learn how to create a product with universal appeal, something that can float in the world mix, rather than feed into the immediate experience of people in their own culture. That package may work for some, as I believe my student's account of dramatic upheavals in the Mongol empire will for many readers; it has its intellectual ideas and universal issues: but it doesn't engage us deeply, as my other student's work might if only he could get it right. And this is not simply an issue of setting the book at home or abroad, but of having it spring from matters that genuinely concern the writer and the culture he's working in.

When, after six months, my Italian students return from England, they have to prepare their thesis, usually a translation of a contemporary novel, complete with accompanying analysis. For this, I tell them, world literature will not be much help. Now they must read as much contemporary Italian writing as possible, whether fiction or nonfiction, journalism or essays, whatever: because it is into this immediate local and contemporary reality, with its ideas, stories, and debates, that the foreign novel they are translating is to be introduced; it is in this restricted national setting, Italy today, that the work must find its place and make sense.

ART THAT STAYS HOME

"IF A BOOK is really good, it will reach out to everyone, the world over," one of the directors of the Edinburgh Book Festival tells me. We're attending a reception at the National Gallery of Scotland to celebrate a loan of nineteen Dutch paintings from the seventeenth century, housed for many years in glorious isolation in a stately home on the Isle of Bute, along with the publication of Dutch writer Herman Koch's new novel, *The Dinner.* The director has been talking to me about the festival's determination to bring foreign authors to Edinburgh—because the best writing should be available everywhere.

"It's interesting," I tell her, "that this belief in the universal appeal of fine literature exactly coincides with commercial convenience. The better a book is, the more it transcends its local origins, the more people it can be sold to worldwide." Put like that, she feels, the position sounds cynical, yet she sincerely believes, and her experience confirms, that the best literary work always transcends borders.

"The other advantage of this approach"—I go on playing devil's advocate, unwisely, since I was one of the authors invited to the festival—is that we never need feel anxious or frustrated that we might be missing out on some truly great work of art because we don't really know the culture that produced it: if the work were really great, it would, by definition, reach out to us; if it doesn't, it's not worth our, nor anyone else's attention. Basically, I can feel confident that I am the arbiter of everything.

At this point, and it's probably just as well, our conversation is interrupted by the evening's scheduled proceedings: the consul for the Netherlands speaks briefly of the Earl of Bute's remarkable art collection and the nineteen Dutch masters on loan to the Scottish museum; Herman Koch's publisher and then Koch himself say a few words about his novel, but really so few that he's hardly started before he's finished. All I can gather is that the book takes place at a dinner party where two Dutch families discuss an outrage committed by their sons and find themselves obliged to choose between protecting their children and remaining true to their humanitarian beliefs.

After the book presentation, people drift off to visit the paintings, which feature a number of artists, in particular Aelbert Cuyp, who was hugely popular with British collectors in the eighteenth century. Cuyp's paintings are rather melancholy, sentimental, quietly elegant representations of cattle in watery landscapes, perhaps with a child cowherd adding a touch of pathos, images that do not appear to require any special knowledge or expertise to decipher.

Other works, apparently less popular among foreign collectors, include far more local and particularly social detail. *The Disputed Reckoning* by Pieter de Hooch shows a behatted man in animated conversation with a drably dressed woman. It takes me a few moments to remember that reckoning is an old word for bill, like the German *Rechnung*: we have two people arguing about cash. That shifts things a little. No doubt if I were more familiar with Dutch mores in the seventeenth century the clothes and the ambience might tell me more, or perhaps even raise a smile.

And all the time I'm looking at the pictures I'm trying to figure out the implications of this idea that important art always travels. One consequence must be that, however deeply a work is immersed in the local and contemporary—like de Hooch's painting of this quarrel over a bill, a hotel bill I'm beginning to think now—recognition of local detail is not essential for appreciating what really matters, which in this case must be the falling out over money of two people, a man and woman, their bodies animated, the woman raising a hand as she leans aggressively toward the man who has his right hand in his pocket, perhaps feeling for coins—assuming people kept coins in their pockets, in Holland, in those times.

The universalist approach, that is, invites us to extrapolate or identify some easily communicable, generic element—unequal power relationships, existential anxieties, or some key idea central to all human life—and tells us that this is what matters about the work of art, not the nature of its engagement with its culture of origin, with the colors of the rooms, the furnishings, the things people wore, or habitual body postures of the time. So in Koch's novel we would be dwelling on the inevitable tension between family loyalty and respect for society's rule of law, or for humanitarian ideals—something understandable all over the world—rather than savoring, from within the experience of Dutch culture, exactly where these families were coming from, how they recall or don't recall things Dutch readers recognize in their Dutch lives.

But what if the quality of some fine works of art lies exactly in their relationship with the local and the contemporary, with the life that it has been given to them to experience here and now? I'm reminded of a telling moment at a conference in 2005 to celebrate the hundredth anniversary of the birth of Henry Green, a novelist who never enjoyed more than a small following, but whose admirers nevertheless tend to make great claims for him, as if the intensity of their enthusiasm had to make up for the author's failure to become a truly major name, or an international figure (for sure, Green's prose does not translate easily).

Invited to give the keynote speech, James Wood kicked off by asking the question, Why did Green remain, for all our affection for him, a minor rather than a major author? This notion caused some consternation among the adoring crowd. Wood went on to conclude that Green's novels, all focused on carefully circumscribed and intensely observed milieu (the servants in a wealthy household in Ireland in the Second World War, a group of spoiled rich people on their way to France caught in a fog in Victoria Station, a middle-class London couple and their small circle of friends in the 1950s), had never posited or dramatized grand moral issues, in the way works by, say, Tolstoy, Dickens, Faulkner, or indeed any "great" novelist, do.

My heart rebelled. Of course Wood was perfectly right: Green didn't pose—or seem remotely interested in posing—grand moral questions. Yet I knew that Green, whatever his national or international reputation, was not minor *for me*; on the contrary his work had been absolutely crucial to forming my sense of the pleasures that might be had from literature. His eccentric mix of empathetic observation, perfect mimicry, but also strangely distorting, sometimes surreal, often hilarious description and commentary, always enchanted me, conveying an urgency of engagement and a subtle complicity that seemed in no way provincial but that required at least some knowledge of the milieu to appreciate. And in these books, you could not set this aspect aside to extrapolate some universal quality, either at the level of a normally satisfying plot, or a philosophical reflection.

Another example of an author in this position might be Barbara Pym, particularly in a late work like *A Few Green Leaves*, where the characters, not one of whom is granted so much as a hint of charisma, allow the great intensities of life to pass them by, taking refuge in, but also suffocated by, the warm wet blanket of social routine in an English village parish. After Pym's death, her work enjoyed a vogue in the United States in the 1980s when she was perceived as a purveyor of English quaintness; yet for an English person reading her fiction, there was nothing quaint about it, rather an invitation to accept that however trivial, a fondness for social minutiae can offer a consolation, or at least a hiding place, when existential winds blow cold.

But again, to engage with this and respond to Pym's wry genius, some familiarity with the milieu is required. I cannot imagine getting the same pleasure from, say, a Burmese Barbara Pym, or even a Spanish Barbara Pym, if such figures were to exist. But I believe Pym and Green to be finer writers than many a worthy Nobel laureate taking in the grand questions of the century. In this regard, it's interesting that Alfred Nobel's will stipulated that the winner of his international literature prize must show "outstanding work in an ideal direction." While it's not quite clear what this might mean, it would seem to suggest some characteristic or principle that can be abstracted from the writing and then mentioned by the jury as a good reason for giving an author the prize: this man's work promotes justice, this woman's writing promotes peace, etc.

I believe this whole approach is limiting and risks obscuring how literature is actually experienced and how it can indeed act positively in our lives, without playing out great moral dramas or drawing us toward weighty opinions. In *Steps to an Ecology of Mind*, discussing a Balinese painting depicting a cremation procession, the British anthropologist Gregory Bateson remarked that you might think the painting was about funeral rituals, or that it portrayed a Balinese tendency to combine grief with gaiety, or alternatively you might notice that by introducing a very large cremation tower that must be carried through a narrow gateway the artist had introduced a bizarre phallic symbol. In fact, Bateson concludes, the more you looked, the more the painting seemed to be an invitation to contemplate the possible relatedness of all these elements and indeed the manner of drawing and coloring in which they were all brought together. The overall effect, he thought, was not to say anything about any of the elements but to draw the mind to a contemplative state where the desire for easy meaning and the consequent purposefulness that comes with believing you have understood something was thwarted by a beautiful complexity, or rather a recognition that life is beautifully complex, beyond easy rational apprehension. Engagement with art, whether it is such a painting, or the interrelatedness of characters and environment in a novel, or the interplay of motifs in music, had the effect of countering what Bateson saw as our dangerous yearning to arrive at a crude understanding of the world and then intervene.

As Bateson saw it, then, the depiction of grand ideals was not necessary to make art that might have a positive influence; on the other hand, an intimate knowledge of the local gave author and audience a chance for a more intense experience of connections, complications, and mysteries. International recognition of this or that hugely superior work of art was not important, nor was a discussion of its supposed ideas; what counted, on the contrary, was a frequent, ongoing experience of art, something that might correct our normally reductive and rapacious ways of thinking.

Let me close by proposing this little experiment. Choose any "great" novel, no more than a century old, from your own home culture; in fact, the nearer to home the better; get on the net and check with a couple of critics what major issues the book articulates, and what profound thoughts make it worthy of the international recognition it enjoys. Then try reading it. A hundred to one the simplicities and dogmatisms of criticism will dissolve in a richness of voice and elusive ethos that is constructed from all the different elements of the culture the writer is bringing together. What you actually experience line by line as the book connects with so much you already know, rearranging it in new ways, or sparking recognitions set off by novelties, is not something that can easily be articulated, or that a foreigner reading the same book in translation will necessarily get.

After a while it may even seem as if those elements that raised the book to its special international status are quite incidental to its real performance, almost an alibi that allowed the work to circulate in a politically correct environment. This was certainly my experience a couple of years ago when I started rereading Thomas Hardy; there is so much more in the texture of his writing, the liveliness of his dialogue playing off against the absorption in landscape, than in any of the famed discussions of fate and destiny. It would be a great shame if we were to lose this intense experience of reading for a product with "an ideal direction" that can more easily be discussed among international audiences at literary festivals.

WRITING WITHOUT STYLE

WHAT IS LITERARY style and why is it bound to change as the novel rapidly goes global?

"Style is the transformation the writer imposes on reality," Proust tells us. We know what he means, perhaps, but the claim hardly helps us describe how a style is created or how it achieves its effects. In fact I can think of no adequate definition of style, if only because it is always diffuse throughout a text. It cannot be pinned down or wrapped up. All the same, we know at once when style is present, especially when it is extreme. Here are the opening lines of Henry Green's 1939 novel *Party Going*:

> Fog was so dense, bird that had been disturbed went flat into a balustrade and slowly fell, dead at her feet.
>
> There it lay and Miss Fellowes looked up to where that pall of fog was twenty foot above and out of which it had fallen, turning over once. She bent down and took a wing then entered a tunnel in front of her, and this had DEPARTURES lit up over it, carrying her dead pigeon.

This is not standard English. The deixis, in particular the combination of dropped articles and unnecessary demonstratives, is wayward. There's something unusual too in the syntax of the opening sentence of the second paragraph: "Miss Fellowes looked up to where that pall of fog was twenty foot above and..." And what? "And very thick," you could say. Or, "and decided to pick up the pigeon." But you can't at this point say, "and out of which...." It's as if two different syntactical structures had been imperfectly aligned around the word *and*, an effect not unlike the breaking up of visual planes in cubism. In general, there is an odd fragmenting of information, and a curious uncertainty about where sentences are going, "turning over once."

It's easy enough to see how this fragmentation links to what is being described: the loss of direction and orientation a fog causes, the idea of departures, both in train stations and in prose. But alongside the disorientation, the alliterative rhythms of the writing suggest purposefulness and solidity. Fog flat fell feet, the first sentence offers, and again, dense bird disturbed balustrade dead. The acoustic effect is intensified by the prevalence of monosyllables and the elimination of unstressed articles, or their substitution with a stressed demonstrative. As in nonsense poetry, if the sense seems odd or uncertain, the forward movement is extremely confident. Here is another sentence playing the same tricks:

> Headlights of cars above turning into a road as they swept round hooting swept their light above where she walked, illuminating lower branches of trees.

So a number of strategies interact in a pattern to create something homogeneous and distinct. You know immediately you are reading

Henry Green. But this doesn't happen in a vacuum. Readers would not notice the text was "special" if they were not expecting something different, something they had seen many times before. There must be a shared understanding of standard language and syntax, a range of more common usages that generally prevail. English readers in particular (as opposed to American) will notice that some of the effects here recall the working-class dialects of northern England, in which articles are often dropped and one says *foot* rather than *feet* when indicating lengths. There's an irony here since Green's novel focuses on London's aristocratic rich, while the third-person narrative voice recalls a working-class north, distant and potentially critical. Yet the voice is not a straight imitation of dialect, since many other dialect elements are missing. In the end, it is not clear what Green's style "means" or where exactly it's coming from, but it does begin to establish, as it were, a position, a new and unusual space, within the known cultural setting of 1930s England.

Style, then, involves a meeting between arrangements inside the prose and expectations outside it. You can't have a strong style without a community of readers able to recognize and appreciate its departures from the common usages they know. Much of what is surprising in Green's text is inevitably lost in translation, in a language, for example, with different rules of deixis; some is lost simply by shifting the book across the Atlantic. Green's work never traveled well.

Perhaps such an extreme example is too easy. Here is F. Scott Fitzgerald, introducing Gatsby's old lover Daisy and her husband, Tom, in *The Great Gatsby*:

Why they came East I don't know. They had spent a year in France, for no particular reason, and then drifted here and there unrestfully wherever people played polo and were rich together. This was a permanent move, said Daisy over the telephone, but I didn't believe it—I had no sight into Daisy's heart but I felt that Tom would drift on forever seeking, a little wistfully, for the dramatic turbulence of some irrecoverable football game.

At first glance this may seem fairly standard prose. But my Word spell-check does underline *unrestfully*, and in fact this word is not in Webster's dictionary. It's a classic case of a word gaining meaning by not being what you expected: They drifted here and there...how? *restlessly*, of course. But *restless* suggests an impulse to be up and doing. It can be a noble attribute. *Unrestfully* suggests not so much the impulse that drives Daisy and Tom to move—actually they only drift—but a lack of benefit from their languor. They drift without relaxing. Fitzgerald feels this mental state is sufficiently special to deserve a neologism to point it up.

But a style requires a combination of interacting elements. What do we have? Well, a reiterated absence of knowledge or meaning: "I don't know." "No particular reason." "I didn't believe." "I had no sight into Daisy's heart." This lack of knowledge might connect up with the repetition of the verb *drift*. One doesn't know where to go, so one drifts. Then, at the heart of the paragraph, there is one strong affirmation of certainty—"This was a permanent move"—but the claim is undermined by a blatant oxymoron, made possible by the double meaning of *move*: "move house" or just movement. To read a few more pages of *The Great Gatsby* would alert us to the fact that the book is full of oxymorons—ferocious indifference, magnanimous scorn, inessential houses—suggesting a general state of precariousness.

Perhaps related to the oxymoron, "permanent move," is the other oddity in this paragraph: "wherever people played polo and were rich together." Standard usage has people being happy together, or sad together: emotional states. Alternatively partners can *get* rich together, or *get* stoned together: progressive developments. But this confusion of an emotional state with a generous bank balance, "were rich together," is emblematic of everything that makes Gatsby's elegant world so oddly fragile, as if it existed only in the magic of words that somehow stick together despite their contradictory energies.

As with Henry Green, much of this is lost when Fitzgerald's text leaves the culture it was written in and travels around the world in other languages. I've looked at five Italian translations of *Gatsby*. None is able to convey "unrestfully," "permanent move," or "get rich together." It's surprising how much trouble they have too with an "irrecoverable football game," a longing for an unrepeatable past that connects Tom with Gatsby and measures the distance between them: Gatsby dreams of reviving love, Tom of reliving sporting glory. And as the separate stylistic devices disappear in translation, so does the pattern that they combined to sustain; losing the pattern one inevitably loses the peculiar position the text created for itself within its culture of origin and hence its special relationship with readers. In translation, stripped of its style, *Gatsby* really doesn't seem a very remarkable performance.

What I'm getting at is that style is predicated on a strict relation to a specific readership and the more that readership is diluted or extended, particularly if it includes foreign-language readers, the more difficult it is for a text of any stylistic density to be successful. In the past, a work of literature would establish a reputation in its culture of origin, first among critics who were presumably equipped to appreciate it, then among the larger public; only later, sometimes many years later, would it perhaps be translated by those cosmopolitan literati who wished to make it known in another country. Now, on the contrary, everything is immediate; the work of a major established author is pronounced a masterpiece the day it is published; translations, even of less celebrated authors like myself, are often prepared for simultaneous publication in a score of countries. In the long run, whether through a growing awareness of the situation on the part of writers, or simply by a process of natural selection, it seems inevitable that style will align with what can be readily translated more or less into multiple languages and cultural settings, or into an easily intelligible international idiom.

In this regard let me mention two recent novels at once very literary and evidently global in their aspirations: Andrés Neuman's *Traveler of the Century*, and the 2013 Booker winner, *The Luminaries*, by the New Zealand writer Eleanor Catton. Neuman, Argentinian, but resident in Spain, sets his work in the early part of the nineteenth century somewhere in Germany (neither date nor place are exactly defined), where a mysterious traveler falls to frequenting the cultural salon of a rich family and deploys his wit to seduce a local and highly intellectual beauty. The register is high, the lexical range considerable, the style extravagantly articulated and playfully pompous; but the knowledge it asks of its reader is all book knowledge, general history, a vague awareness of what a high prose style once was. There is no appeal to anything writer and reader know and share in the here and now, though we do get some softly eroticized, politically correct enthusiasm for internationalism.

This is what our mysterious traveler talks to his beloved about when they are at last between the sheets:

> How can we speak about free trade, Hans pronounced as he lay next to Sophie, of a customs union and all that implies, without considering a free exchange of literature? We should be translating as many foreign books as possible, publishing them, reclaiming the literature of other countries and taking it to the

classroom! That's what I told Brockhaus. And what did he say? Sophie asked, nibbling his nipple. Hans shrugged and stroked her back: He told me, yes, all in good time, and not to get agitated. But in such exchanges, said Sophie, it's important that the more powerful countries don't impose their literature on everyone else, don't you think? Absolutely, replied Hans, plunging his hand between Sophie's buttocks, and besides, powerful countries have a lot to learn from smaller countries which are usually more open and curious, that is to say more knowledgeable. You're the curious one! Sophie sighed, allowing Hans's probing finger in and lying back. That, Hans grinned, must be because you're so open and you know what's what.

Reviewing *The Luminaries*, an eight-hundred-page mystery story set in 1860s New Zealand, Catton's compatriot C. K. Stead remarks on its "chintzy," "upholstered" pastiche of the nineteenth-century novel and adds:

Every episode has its setting, decor, clothing, its period bric-a-brac, its slightly formal but often sharp dialogue. This is costume drama. It is conventional fiction but with the attention to fact and connection that the (cross-checking and online research) facilities of the modern computer permit. That apart, only the author's cultural sensitivity in dealing with Maori and Chinese characters, and an occasional anachronistic word or phrase in the dialogue ("paranoid", "serendipitous") locate authorship in the present.

In general terms this would also be an appropriate description of Neuman's book. Removing us from the present, pastiching what the modern ear assumes the eloquence of the past to have been, the writer can appear "stylish" without appealing to anything in his reader-ship's immediate experience. Catton's prose has been likened to that of Dickens in *The Pickwick Papers*. But for readers who followed it in the 1830s, *Pickwick* was drenched in references to the world they shared, and the language itself was not so far away from what could be heard and read every day. If one translates Dickens into another language, an enormous amount is lost; even for the Londoner read-ing him today, half the references mean nothing. Neuman's and Cat-ton's novels have dispensed in advance with this intense engagement with a local or national readership and seem set to lose very little as they move around the world in different languages. It is in this regard alone that one has to disagree with Stead. Authorship *is* located in the present exactly insofar as its appeal—as in a Hollywood costume drama or indeed an extravagant computer game—is to well-estab-lished, globally shared tropes and not to any real contact with the specificity of a here and now.

LITERATURE AND BUREAUCRACY

I AM CURRENTLY involved in two huge projects: one to give the Italian government an absolutely exhaustive description of the degree course in which I teach and one to give the same, but in response to a different set of questions and assumptions, to the European Commission. We are talking hundreds of pages and hours upon hours that could far more usefully be spent helping students, correcting their essays, and preparing lessons. Needless to say my university is not alone in devoting time to such activities. Nor are universities special in this regard. Nor is Italy, where I live, for all its genius for bureaucracy, any worse than the UK or the USA in this matter (indeed my dealings with both the States and Britain suggests those countries may be worse). What we have then is a propensity in modern life to substitute cataloguing and recording for actual doing, to create for ourselves an illusion of responsible action by endlessly multiplying the work, so-called, that *precedes* and—in the rare cases where it actually occurs—follows responsible action.

Literature, of course, is implacably opposed to bureaucracy. Isn't it? Here is Dickens in *Little Dorrit* (the chapter is called "CONTAINING THE WHOLE SCIENCE OF GOVERNMENT") castigating the

British Treasury Office, which he renames the Circumlocution Office:

> The Circumlocution Office was (as everybody knows without being told) the most important Department under Government. No public business of any kind could possibly be done at any time without the acquiescence of the Circumlocution Office. Its finger was in the largest public pie, and in the smallest public tart. It was equally impossible to do the plainest right and to undo the plainest wrong without the express authority of the Circumlocution Office. If another Gunpowder Plot had been discovered half an hour before the lighting of the match, nobody would have been justified in saving the parliament until there had been half a score of boards, half a bushel of minutes, several sacks of official memoranda, and a family-vault full of ungrammatical correspondence, on the part of the Circumlocution Office.
>
> This glorious establishment had been early in the field, when the one sublime principle involving the difficult art of governing a country, was first distinctly revealed to statesmen. It had been foremost to study that bright revelation and to carry its shining influence through the whole of the official proceedings. Whatever was required to be done, the Circumlocution Office was beforehand with all the public departments in the art of perceiving—HOW NOT TO DO IT.

For a dozen pages the concept of how not to do something and the mysteries of this policy's universal "implementation" are thoroughly explored. Some of the observations will be all too familiar to anyone living in a democracy:

It is true that every new premier and every new government, coming in because they had upheld a certain thing as necessary to be done, were no sooner come in than they applied their utmost faculties to discovering How not to do it. It is true that from the moment when a general election was over, every returned man who had been raving on hustings because it hadn't been done, and who had been asking the friends of the honorable gentleman in the opposite interest on pain of impeachment to tell him why it hadn't been done, and who had been asserting that it must be done, and who had been pledging himself that it should be done, began to devise, How it was not to be done. It is true that the debates of both Houses of Parliament the whole session through, uniformly tended to the protracted deliberation, How not to do it. It is true that the royal speech at the opening of such session virtually said, My lords and gentlemen, you have a considerable stroke of work to do, and you will please to retire to your respective chambers, and discuss, How not to do it. It is true that the royal speech, at the close of such session, virtually said, My lords and gentlemen, you have through several laborious months been considering with great loyalty and patriotism, How not to do it, and you have found out; and with the blessing of Providence upon the harvest (natural, not political), I now dismiss you. All this is true, but the Circumlocution Office went beyond it.

Dickens was not the only one to launch such attacks. It's hard to think of a major writer—Tolstoy, Dostoevsky, Balzac, Zola, Flaubert, Kafka, Joyce, Lawrence—who hasn't at some point or other satirized bureaucracy. So why has such writing produced no results? This is Orwell, himself no mean satirist of the British civil service, commenting on Dickens:

In *Oliver Twist*, *Hard Times*, *Bleak House*, *Little Dorrit*, Dickens attacked English institutions with a ferocity that has never since been approached. Yet he managed to do it without making himself hated, and, more than this, the very people he attacked have swallowed him so completely that he has become a national institution himself. In its attitude towards Dickens the English public has always been a little like the elephant which feels a blow with a walking-stick as a delightful tickling. Before I was ten years old I was having Dickens ladled down my throat by schoolmasters in whom even at that age I could see a strong resemblance to Mr. Creakle, and one knows without needing to be told that lawyers delight in Sergeant Buzfuz and that *Little Dorrit* is a favourite in the Home Office. Dickens seems to have succeeded in attacking everybody and antagonizing nobody. Naturally this makes one wonder whether after all there was something unreal in his attack upon society.

Orwell treats Dickens as if he were a special case, but the question he raises here is whether all satire isn't to some extent in connivance with the object of its attacks. After all, hasn't Orwell's own *1984* become almost an official text in the country that has more surveillance cameras per citizen than any other in the world? Leaving England, the Austrian writer Thomas Bernhard, another ferocious critic of his state, became fascinated by the extent to which people actually lapped up the criticism, applauded him for berating them. In the play *Am Ziel* (which might be translated *Arrived*) the lead character, who is simply designated The Writer, remarks of his successful play:

I can't understand
why they applauded
we are talking about a play

that exposes every one of them
and in the meanest way
admittedly with humor
but nasty humor
if not with malice
true malice
And all of a sudden they applaud.[1]

Years later, commenting on the controversy surrounding Bernhard, the East German playwright Heiner Müller said, "He writes as if he had been hired by the Austrian government to write against Austria. . . . The disturbance can be articulated that loudly and clearly because it doesn't disturb."

So could it be—and this is the question I really want to ask—that however much literature may appear to be opposed to bureaucracy and procrastination, it actually partakes of the same aberration? Balzac's *Comedie humaine* with his declared ambition to "compete with the civil registry"; Proust's monstrous, magnificent *Recherche*, which he likened to a cathedral, tediously extending the analogy to every section of the work; Joyce's encyclopedic aspirations in *Ulysses*, his claim that *Finnegans Wake* would be a history of the entire world. Or go back to Dante, if you like, and his need to find a pigeonhole in hell for every sinner of every category from every sphere of society. Or fast forward again to Bouvard and Pécuchet, Flaubert's two incompetents who react to practical failure by becoming obsessive copiers of literary snippets. This without mentioning the contenders for the Great-American-Novel slot, so eager to give the impression that their minds have encompassed and interrelated everything across

---

1. Translation by Gitta Honegger in her biography, *Thomas Bernhard: The Making of an Austrian*, Yale University Press, 2001, p. 36.

that enormous continent (one thinks of the interminable lists of contemporary paraphernalia in Jonathan Franzen's writing). In each case, however different in tone and content the texts, life is transformed into a series of categories, made more mental, more a matter of words and intellect; we revel in the mind's ability to possess the world in language, rather than to inhabit it or change it.

And of course all these literary achievements are wonderful and "enriching" (as they say) and infinitely more attractive than the dull documents I and my colleagues are compiling to describe our degree course to the European Commission; nevertheless they share with that document and with the people who devised it the desire for a control that stands off from participation, and perhaps substitutes for it. Similarly, the windy length of Dickens's denunciation of the Circumlocution Office, and the lingering pleasure he evidently takes in blowing it away, share that office's sinister vocation, which is why, as Orwell says, the bureaucrats themselves recognize and love the spirit of the passage. One almost feels it's worth having a Circumlocution Office so Dickens can describe it. A dangerous state of mind.

The question arises: Is all locution inevitably circumlocution (as Beckett tended to think), and will the West perhaps slowly and voluptuously choke itself in a mounting tangle of red tape, meantime entertaining itself to death with a mountain of literature that describes and charmingly castigates the whole scandalous process? Wouldn't it be strange, in the end, if there were not a continuity of vocation between these two major facets of the same culture? Here am I, after all, writing about other people writing about things, and with a little luck someone writing somewhere else will castigate me for my cynicism and irresponsibility, since we all know that literature, like democracy (and most of all the British democracy that gave us the Circumlocution Office), must always be praised to high heaven.

IN THE CHLOROFORMED SANCTUARY

"WALK AROUND A university campus," fumes Geoff Dyer in *Out of Sheer Rage*, "and there is an almost palpable smell of death about the place because hundreds of academics are busy killing everything they touch." Is Dyer correct that while original literature throbs with life, literary criticism is the work of cloistered drudges who suffocate the very creature that provides them with a living?

At least on this score reviewers can be quickly exonerated; it may be miles away from facing and firing bullets, or performing open heart surgery, but reviewing does have an immediate impact on other people's lives. Panning or praising a novel, the reviewer is aware he is administering pain or pleasure and that quite possibly there will be a reaction, as when Jeanette Winterson turned up on a reviewer's doorstep to berate him in person for a poor review. One celebrated novelist who felt I had reviewed him unkindly spent an hour making a transatlantic phone call to my own publisher to complain about my wickedness. A reviewer fearful of the fray would be well advised to find another job.

Not so the academic critic. While the reviewer is generally freelance and may hope to increase his or her income through a policy of lively provocation and polemics, the academic, though hardly well off, is more reliably salaried within a solid university institution. Rather than being part of the market with the obvious function of swaying reader's purchasing choices, these critics treat literature as an object of quasi-scientific research. They're not obliged to entertain, but then nor is there any question of their findings being used to propose any program of improvement; they needn't fear the moment when their work is measured against reality. In short, the academic critic's task is purely one of exegesis and clarification. So it may come as a surprise to those unfamiliar with this kind of writing how frequently it resorts to a jargon and manner that guarantees ordinary consumers of literature will be repelled.

Here are three typical passages, none of them extreme, the first pulled (at random) from an essay by Paul Davies in *The Cambridge Companion to Beckett*:

> From its first words, then, *Comment c'est* acknowledges the aesthetic of recommencement that Beckett had already developed with such compaction in *Texts*. Working together, these two projects carry out the wisdom of the pun: "commencer" is "comment c'est." Beginning again, he returns again. Commencing, he quotes. As I argued above, it was the insistence of this insight that had led Beckett in the *Texts* to the strategic deployment of the gap between texts. These twelve gaps were in their turn yet another seed for *How it is*. They grew into roughly eight-hundred-and-twenty-five gaps, each of which, as John Pilling has pointed out, enabled a formal re-enactment of the book's inception.

Here, equally at random from the shelves beside my desk, is Amit Chaudhuri writing about Lawrence's poems in *Birds, Beasts and Flowers*:

What is agreed upon generally then is that, to appropriate a term from linguistics, the "signified" of the poem is undefinable, powerful, ineffable, but mysteriously transmissible and even paraphrasable. This "signified" which may be called "otherness" or "life," lies outside the text, out there in the landscape or object described, while each signifier—bat, snake, eagle, tortoise, fish—makes a connection with the "signified," thus capturing, conveying or evoking it.

Finally, from the realm of translation criticism, this is Lawrence Venuti, in *Rethinking Translation*, talking about Iginio Tarchetti's nineteenth-century Italian "adaptations" of stories by Mary Shelley:

Yet Shelley's authorship comes back to worry the ideological standpoint of Tarchetti's intervention by raising the issue of gender. To be effective as a subversion of bourgeois values which deterritorializes the Italian literary standard, his text must maintain the fiction of his authorship, referring to Shelley's tale only in the vaguest way ('imitation'). At the same time, however this fiction suppresses an instance of female authorship so that the theft of Shelley's literary creation has the patriarchal effect of female disempowerment, of limiting a woman's social agency.

All three of these pieces contain useful, almost "common sense" observations on the texts they are talking about. Yet this common sense is made to seem arduous through the use of unnecessary jargon. There is also a solemnity that combines with the ugliness of style to push the writing toward bathos. I suspect Davies's metaphor of "twelve gaps" being "a seed" that "grew into *roughly* eight-hundred-and-twenty-five gaps" would have had Beckett laughing out loud.

The mix of intellectual control and creeping tedium goes hand in hand with a focus on the arcane rather than the evident; technique rather than content. Areas where the critic can claim special expertise are stressed, while a book's part in the writer's life is played down, as if for fear that any layman might feel he had the right to discuss such matters. Academics are naturally attracted to the kind of writer whose flaunted complexity offers scope for that expertise, rather than one taking on his material in a more direct fashion. So Joyce is infinitely preferred to Chesterton (in passing it's interesting that Borges, himself the object of endless academic criticism, preferred Chesterton to Joyce).

What is in it for these critics? They stake out a field in which only a relatively small group of initiates can compete; their writing is safe from public scrutiny, it threatens no one and can do little damage; at the same time they may enjoy the illusion of possessing, encompassing, and even somehow neutralizing the most sparkling and highly regarded creations of the imagination.

This is what Dyer so comically hates in *Out of Sheer Rage*. Here he is opening the *Longman Critical Reader* to his favorite author, D. H. Lawrence:

> I glanced at the contents page: old Eagleton was there, of course, together with some other state-of-the-fart theorists: Lydia Blanchard on "Lawrence, Foucault and the Language of Sexuality" (in the section on "Gender, Sexuality, Feminism"), Daniel J. Schneider on "Alternatives to Logocentrism in D. H. Lawrence" (in the section featuring "Post-Structuralist Turns"). I could feel myself getting angry and then I flicked through the introductory essay on "Radical Indeterminacy: A Post-Modern Lawrence" and became angrier still. How could it have hap-

pened? How could these people with no feeling for literature have ended up teaching it, writing about it?

But is Dyer really angry? Is he angry for the reasons he says he is? Might it not be that the creative writer, conflicted over issues of fear and courage (Dyer seems terribly eager to demonstrate that his own writing is alive, engaged, and courageous) is actually a little envious of the academic who is perfectly happy to retreat from life into the chloroformed sanctuary of academe and makes no pretense at all of being in the front line?

Or, alternatively, could it be that the creative writer is delighted to find in the evident dullness of academic criticism a kind of writing in comparison with which his or her own work will inevitably seem vital and exciting? Dyer is wonderfully alive and engaged as he lets rip at the academics, "this group of wankers huddled in a circle, backs turned to the world so that no one would see them pulling each other off."

At this point you might begin to think that the secret purpose of dusty, phobic academe is to reassure the insecure "creative" writers of their own liveliness. This "vast graveyard of dust," as Dyer would have it, is a place you visit to congratulate yourself you're still up in the sunshine. It is also a very soft target. Nobody need be afraid, attacking academe, that the critics will lash back, or that they could hurt much if they did. Indeed the idea that academic critics "kill" literature tells us more about Dyer's lively imagery than about the critics' lethal powers. These men are hardly killers. If there's an assassin here, it's the creative writer. At worst the academics will tuck an author to sleep in mothballs. We can enjoy getting a whiff of camphor and feel superior.

For myself, I've written too many novels, plenty of reviews, and an academic monograph on translation and literature. Reviewing, I try to say what I think without actually being offensive. Writing fiction, I try not to worry how offensive the reviewers might be to me. Writing academic criticism—a ticket-punching necessity if one wishes to teach at a university—I'm relieved, of course, that offense and abrasion just don't come into it, but immediately anxious that no one cares what I write in this department; life is passing me by.

But here's a conundrum to close on. If, in response to Dyer's claim that there is "an almost palpable smell of death" about university campuses, a critic were to remark that "almost palpable" is nonsense—in that you can either smell something or you can't and if you can't how could you know that you almost could?—would that critic be against life, because he was pedantically deflating Dyer's lively rant? Or would he be on the side of life because he was reminding us of how things really are and what the words actually mean? Certainly the campus where I teach is full of young people, often in each other's arms, usually far too busy with life to be bothered about literature. The only musty smells are in the library stacks.

WRITERS INTO SAINTS

THE GREATEST, THE best, the finest, the most innovative, the most perceptive...

Over the last ten years or so I have read literary biographies of Dickens, Dostoevsky, Chekhov, Hardy, Leopardi, Verga, Lawrence, Joyce, Woolf, Moravia, Morante, Malaparte, Pavese, Borges, Beckett, Bernhard, Christina Stead, Henry Green, and probably others too. With only the rarest of exceptions, and even then only for a page or two, each author is presented as simply the most gifted and well-meaning of writers, while their behavior, however problematic and possibly outrageous—Dickens's treatment of his children, Lawrence's fisticuffs with Frieda—is invariably seen in a flattering light. We're not quite talking hagiography, but special pleading is everywhere evident, as if biographers were afraid that the work might be diminished by a life that was less than noble or not essentially directed toward a lofty cause.

Consider Hermione Lee on Woolf's suicide: the biographer takes it as an indication of Woolf's resilience and courage for *not* having committed suicide in the preceding years, despite her severe depression—a courage directed at breakthroughs in fiction on behalf of female emancipation and for the general furtherance of our culture.

There is no real basis for this reflection, or any need for it. Lee simply takes whatever chances she can to build up a positive moral image of Woolf.

Gordon Bowker takes Joyce at his word that he had to leave Ireland because he was unable to become a great writer in a provincial atmosphere amid competing claims of nationalism and Catholicism. Yet the facts suggest Joyce was working well in Ireland; he was publishing and had a growing reputation. A more urgent problem was Nora, his uneducated and very young girlfriend whom he was embarrassed to present to family or intellectual friends as his partner, but with whom he wanted to enjoy nuptial bliss at once. That was possible only by moving abroad, a move that definitely slowed down his career and would condition all his work from then on. Bowker enthusiastically recycles the myth of the independent artist seeking alone the "spiritual liberation of his country," then lets us know that Joyce was consulting his aunt by post over his young wife's depression (Nora was desperately lonely in countries where she could not speak the language) and visiting prostitutes in the meantime.

All biographies of Beckett speak with awe of his artistic integrity, his unwillingness to give interviews or to have his novels entered for prizes. But elsewhere it's clear that Beckett had problems with all forms of social engagement, and in particular anything that laid him under an obligation or limited his freedom in any way. In early adulthood he would not work, insisted on his parents' supporting him, but refused to accept that this gave them any right to tell him what to do with his time. Later, he found in his companion, Suzanne Deschevaux-Dumesnil, someone who not only supported him financially but also promoted his work and wrote letters to his publishers for him. In his first novel, *Murphy*, the eponymous hero refuses to work and is supported by a prostitute, though the person he most admires is an autistic patient totally secure from outside influence. In his short story "First Love," a tramp is picked up by a prostitute and taken back to her house for sex. He escapes into a back room, barricades himself in, and asks to be fed and have his chamber pot removed while conceding nothing in return. In neither work is there any question that this withdrawal is done for art or out of a need for integrity.

I deeply admire the work of all these writers. I have no desire to run them down. On the contrary. What I find odd is that biographers apparently feel a need to depict their subjects as especially admirable human beings, something that in the end makes the lives less rather than more interesting and harder rather than easier to relate to the writing. It is so much clearer why the books were written and why they had to be the way they are if the life is given without this constant positive spin.

The tendency may be most pronounced in biographies of Dickens. Quite apart from the writer's dramatic rejection, expulsion even, of his wife after she had given him ten children, there is simply an enormous resistance to admitting what a tyrant the man was, seeking to control the lives of those around him to an extraordinary degree, deeply disappointed and punitive when they didn't live up to his expectations, which was almost always, yet at the same time fearful of any sign of competition. Robert Gottlieb, in *Great Expectations: The Sons and Daughters of Charles Dickens*, is sublime: to let Dickens off one hook he quotes previous biographer and Dickens descendant Lucinda Hawksley as claiming that the author discouraged his son Walter Landor from writing because he was "probably aware 'that [Walter] did not have the aptitude or ambition to work at [it] as hard as he would need to in order to succeed financially.'" At this point the boy, who after all had been named after a poet, was not even in his teens. The fact is that, having styled himself "the Inimitable One," Dickens never wanted competition from his children.

The habit of imagining the writer as more well-meaning than he or she probably was is even more curious when we turn to academe. Usually hostile to any notion that knowledge of a writer's life illuminates his work—"Biographical Fallacy!" one professor of mine would thunder—academic critics nevertheless tend to assume that the author is a solemn soul devoted to profound aesthetic enquiries and invariably progressive narratives. So for Linda Shires, in *Tess of the D'Urbervilles*, Thomas Hardy was "educating his readers by defamiliarization," something that "is the primary goal of a novelist who would have us treat women differently, alter linguistic conventions, and reform the institutions that misshape women as much as language." While for Paul Davies, Beckett "veritably hunted realism to death," where realism is understood to be the convention underpinning bourgeois complacency.

This is biography, not criticism. We are being told of a plan the author had to improve the world. Unfortunately, Shires's remarks give us no sense of why *Tess* is such an absorbing read, nor does any careful attention to the life or indeed the book suggest that this is what is really going on in the writing. It's true that Hardy said he wanted "to demolish the doll of English fiction," but what he was talking about was the freedom of the writer to evoke the lure and terror of sexual experience.

As for Beckett, it is truly hard to see his work as politically motivated. His manner of relating to others in his personal life and in print is to say something and immediately unsay it, declare and then deny. Again and again in the novels he builds up a credibly realistic scene, then steps rapidly away from it: "There's a choice of images!" remarks Malone, having offered us a moving description of his hero Saposcat. His words "went dead as soon as they sounded," says Murphy's girlfriend of Murphy. In his strangely contorted letters to Duthuit, after championing a form of expression free from all relation to the world, Beckett warns: "Bear in mind that I who hardly ever talk about myself talk about little else." In the end, the image he uses to clarify this conundrum is excretion: his writing is something he shits or vomits. He produces it, *has to* produce it, it is *of* him, but it is not about anything nor purposefully meant, and he wishes to push it away from himself as soon as possible—a sort of enactment of self-loathing. This is a fascinating pronouncement on the creative process (Byron said something similar), but hardly the description of a noble task.

Returning then to these overgenerous biographies, and to the constant insinuation of academe that writers are talented laborers in a good cause, one can only assume that they are satisfying a general need to reinforce a positive conception of narrative art, thus bolstering the self-esteem of readers, and even more of critics and biographers, who in writing about literature are likewise contributing to the very same good causes. Authors themselves, though often contradicting this positive image in private (Dickens frequently acknowledged that certain negative characters in his books were based on himself), soon learn how to play the part. Beckett must have been aware of how those famous author photos, suggesting a lean, suffering asceticism, fed the public's perception of an austere and virtuous separateness. "How easy," wrote Beckett's friend Emil Cioran, "to imagine him...in a naked cell, undisturbed by the least decoration, not even a crucifix." Actually Beckett was sharing a spacious flat in central Paris with his lifetime companion, Suzanne, spending weekends and summers with her in their country cottage, but drinking heavily with friends (never Suzanne) most evenings and generally making time for mistresses when possible.

But let's finish with Faulkner's Nobel Prize acceptance speech, a masterpiece in having it both ways: "I feel this award was not made to me as a man," he begins with apparent humility, seemingly denying personal prowess and heading off, as Faulkner always did, the all-too-evident relations between his stories and his biography, "but to my work, a life's work in the agony and sweat of the human spirit." All the attention must be on the work, but as a manifestation of saintly human endeavor. Whose? Faulkner's of course.

III
The Writer's World

THE WRITER'S JOB

WHEN WAS IT exactly that becoming a writer started to be seen as a career choice, with appropriate degree courses and pecking orders? Does this state of affairs make any difference to what gets written?

At school we were taught two opposing visions of the writer as artist. He might be a skilled craftsman bringing his talent to the service of the community, which rewarded him with recognition and possibly money. This, they told us, was the classical position, as might be found in the Greece of Sophocles, or Virgil's Rome, or again in Pope's Augustan Britain. Alternatively the writer might make his or, by now, her own life narrative into art, indifferent to the strictures and censure of society but admired by it precisely because of a refusal to kowtow. This was the Romantic position as it developed in the late eighteenth and nineteenth centuries.

Let's leave aside how accurate this is historically; it's what they taught us and it got stuck in our heads: on the one hand the writer as artisan whose personality was hardly important, the prevalent situation in preindustrial times, when writers were few and held subordinate roles in fairly rigid hierarchies (a Petrarch or a Chaucer); on the other the writer as a charismatic superman (the Byrons and Shelleys) whose refined sensibility and creative powers gave him the right to transgress and question his community's rules. This vision suited a time of tension between individual and mechanized mass society. The Romantic writer helped the reader fight back against the homogenizing pressures of a modern industrialized world.

As we know, T. S. Eliot rather complicated matters by telling us that writers had to overcome their personalities and find a place in the literary tradition; their work would only be truly distinctive when it marked the next development in the natural unfolding of the collective imagination as manifested in "the canon." To the perplexed adolescent I was when I read Eliot, this sophisticated consideration seemed to offer a compromise between the classical and Romantic positions. But only at first glance. Read carefully, Eliot was more Romantic than ever: only those who had real personality, special people like himself, would appreciate what a burden personality was and wish to shed it. For these special people, literature became the drama of the sublimation or sacrifice of self through exploration of the work of other equally special people who came before them, to whose achievements they then added their own individual contributions. There was something painful and noble about this endeavor that raised the writer to a pantheon worshiped by an elite. Above all Eliot stressed that the creation of literature would require endless hard work over many years and quite probably a degree in the classics and/or modern European literatures. The young aspirant now had a core curriculum to follow to become a writer, but knew that it would require many years of hard labor.

Still, none of this prepared us for the advent of creative writing as a "career." In the last thirty or forty years, writers have had to become people who travel along a well-defined career track, like any other middle-class professionals, not, however, to become craftsmen serving the community, but to project an image of themselves (partly through published work, but also in dozens of other ways) as artists who embody the direction in which culture is headed. In short, the next big new thing. A Doris Lessing. Rushdie. A Pamuk.

It's rather as if the spontaneous Romanticism of the nineteenth-century poets had become a job description; we know what a romantic is (the politics, the behavior patterns), we know that is the way to literary greatness, so let's do it. Coetzee's novel *Youth* captures with fine wryness the trials of a methodical young man seeking to make a career out of becoming the kind of writer he is not.

Let's consider a few of the changes that led us to this state of affairs.

In the twentieth century people stopped just reading novels and poems and started studying them. It was a revolution. Suddenly everybody studied literature. At school it was obligatory. They did literature exams. They understood that when there are metaphors and patterns of symbolism and character development, etc., then you have "literature." They supposed that if you could analyze it, you could very probably do it yourself. Since enormous prestige was afforded to writers, and since it was now accepted that nobody needed to be tied to dull careers by such accidents of birth as class, color, sex, or even IQ, large numbers of people (myself included!) began to write. These people felt they knew what literature was and how to make it.

In the second half of the century, the cost of publishing fell considerably, the number of fiction and poetry titles per annum shot up (about one hundred thousand English-language fiction titles are now published worldwide each year), profits were squeezed, discounting was savage. A situation was soon reached where a precious few authors sold vast numbers of books while vast numbers of writers sold precious few books. Such however was the now towering and indeed international celebrity of the former that the latter threw themselves even more eagerly into the fray, partly because they needed their shrinking advances more often, partly in the hope of achieving such celebrity themselves.

It became clear that the task of writers was not just to deliver books, but to promote themselves in every possible way. He, or let's say she, launches a website, a Facebook page (I'm no exception), perhaps hires her own publicist. She attends literary festivals all over the world, for no payment. She sits on literary-prize juries for very little money, writes articles in return for a one-line mention of her recent publication, completes dozens of Internet interviews, offers endorsements for the books of fellow writers in the hope that the compliment will be returned. It would not be hard to add to this list.

In the first half of the twentieth century the decline of the gentleman publisher coincided with a rapid growth in the number of writers seeking to storm the citadel. Along with the increasing complexity of book contracts—hardbacks and paperbacks, bookclubs, bonuses, options, sliding scales of royalties, film rights, foreign rights, territorial divisions, remainders, and a host of other niceties—these conditions created and consolidated the figure of the literary agent.

The emergence of the agent signaled an awareness of a clash between the idea of writing as a romantic, anti-establishment vocation and the need for the professional writer to mesh with a well-established industrial and promotional machine. Hopefully the agent would reconcile the two. Soon, however, agents found themselves so overwhelmed by pressure from would-be new arrivals and contract complications that they could no longer be seen either as a gateway into the world of publishing, or as middle men who could spare writers from getting their hands dirty. It was at this point, in the 1980s, that the creative writing course took off and the figure of the career writer began to assert itself.

One of the myths about creative writing programs is that students enter them to learn how to write. Such learning, when and if it takes place, is a felicitous by-product that may or may not have to do with the teaching; the process of settling down to write for a year would very probably yield results even without teachers. No, the students enter the program to show themselves to teachers who as writers are well placed (they imagine!) to help them present themselves to the publishers. Most creative writing programs now offer classes on approaching agents and publishers and promoting one's work. In short, preparing for the job.

At the same time the perceived need for an expensive yearlong creative writing course on the part of thousands of would-be writers affords paid employment to those older writers who have trouble making ends meet but are nevertheless determined to keep at it. One of the problems of seeing creative writing as a career is that careers are things you go on with till retirement. The fact that creativity may not be co-extensive with one's whole working life is not admitted. A disproportionate number of poets teach in these programs.

Creative writing programs are frequently blamed for a growing standardization and flattening in contemporary narrative. This is unfair. It is the anxiety of the writers about being excluded from their chosen career, together with a shared belief that we know what literature is and can learn how to produce it that encourages people to write similar books. Nobody is actually expecting anything very new. Just new versions of the old. Again and again when reading for review, or doing jury service perhaps for a prize, I come across carefully written novels that "do literature" as it is known. Literary fiction has become a genre like any other, with a certain trajectory, a predictable pay-off, and a fairly limited and well-charted body of liberal Western wisdom to purvey. Much rarer is the sort of book (one thinks of Gerbrand Bakker's *The Twin*, or Peter Stamm's *On a Day Like This*, or going back a way, *Letty Fox: Her Luck*, by the marvelous Australian writer Christina Stead) where the writer appears, amazingly, to be working directly from experience and imagination, drawing on knowledge of past literature only insofar as it offers tools for having life happen on the page.

So then, a would-be anticonventional public enjoys the notion of the rebel, or at least admirably independent, writer, but more and more that same writer, to achieve success, has to tune in to the logic of an industrial machine, which in turn encourages the cultivation of an anticonventional image. This is an incitement to hypocrisy. Meantime the world opens up; books travel further and translate faster than they ever did in the past. A natural selection process favors those writers whose style and content cross borders easily. Success and celebrity breed imitators. Lots of them. Nobody can read everything. Nobody can read the hundredth part of everything. Nevertheless international prizes purport to tell us which is the best novel of the year, who the greatest writer.

The ultimate achievement of the career writer, after a lifetime of literary festivals, shortlists and prizes, readings, seminars, honorary degrees, lectures, and, of course, writing, is, or would be, to place oneself inside "the canon." But in the publishing culture we have today, any idea that a process of slow sifting might produce a credible canon such as those we inherited from the distant past is nonsense. Whatever in the future masquerades as a canon for our own time will largely be the result of good marketing, self-promotion, and pure chance.

Is all this bad news? Only if one is attached to dreams of greatness. In a droll lecture entitled "Ten Thousand Poets" delivered at the annual conference of the Association of Literary Scholars and Critics at Boston University last October, the excellent poet Mark Halliday reflected:

I think all of us who keep striving and striving to publish an-other and another book of poems are still in love with the ideas of GREATNESS and IMPORTANCE.

As Halliday concluded, such ideas were simply not compatible with the era of the career writer.

WRITING TO WIN

ONE OF THE great mysteries of the writer's life is the transformation that occurs when he or she passes from being an unpublished to a published novelist. If you are looking for a textbook case, check out the career of Salman Rushdie. Here he is interviewed in *The Paris Review* in 2005:

> Many people in that very gifted generation I was a part of had found their ways as writers at a much younger age. It was as if they were zooming past me. Martin Amis, Ian McEwan, Julian Barnes, William Boyd, Kazuo Ishiguro, Timothy Mo, Angela Carter, Bruce Chatwin—to name only a few. It was an extraordinary moment in English literature, and I was the one left in the starting gate, not knowing which way to run. That didn't make it any easier.

It's a competition. Pick up a copy of Rushdie's memoir *Joseph Anton* (the pseudonym that aligns Rushdie with two of the greatest writers of modern times) and you find that almost every relationship, whether it be with friends and rivals at school, with his wives and partners, with fellow writers, and finally with the world of Islam, is seen in terms of winning and losing. And at the painful core of these struggles, at least early on, is "his repeated failures to be, or become, a decent publishable writer of fiction." This is the competition of competitions. Publication. Eventually, Rushdie decides that this failure is tied up with an identity question and "slowly, from his ignominious place at the bottom of the literary barrel, he began to understand . . ."

He sets off to India to reinforce the Indian side of his identity because he perceives this will help him to become a successful writer, and indeed soon conceives "a gigantic, all or nothing project" in which "the risk of failure was far greater than the possibility of success." After the publication of *Midnight's Children*, "many things happened about which he had not even dared to dream, awards, bestsellerdom and on the whole, popularity." Of the night when he was awarded the Booker he speaks of his pleasure in opening the "handsome, leatherbound presentation copy of *Midnight's Children*" with "the bookplate inside that read WINNER."

This is what it is about. One reads Rushdie's novels and finds that the major characters, like their creator, tend to be locked into struggles about winning, losing, and general self-aggrandizement: Ormus Cama, for example, hero of *The Ground Beneath Her Feet*, is as desperate to become a rock star as Rushdie was to become a writer. He is also determined to win the beautiful and talented Vina, who despite affection for him sees acceptance of his offer of love as a form of capitulation, eager as she is to have a singing career at least as great as his. Meantime Rai Merchant, the narrator of the novel, competes with Ormus for Vina's affections. *The Satanic Verses* also fields two protagonists both seeking success and celebrity, with the more Rushdie-like of them winning the day.

But more than the plots, Rushdie's constantly crackling language, full of puns and games, and the unrelenting erudition, rapidly establishes a hierarchy that has the writer/narrator dominant and the reader reduced to supine admiration, or if not, irritated. These are the only two responses. On many occasions in *Joseph Anton*, Rushdie expresses genuine puzzlement as to why he has so many enemies among reviewers and fellow authors. More than other winners, he feels. Perhaps it is because he makes it so clear just how important being seen to be a winner is.

On this, alas, he is right. No one is treated with more patronizing condescension than the unpublished author or, in general, the would-be artist. At best he is commiserated. At worst mocked. He has presumed to rise above others and failed. I still recall a conversation around my father's deathbed when the visiting doctor asked him what his three children were doing. When he arrived at the last and said young Timothy was writing a novel and wanted to become a writer, the good lady, unaware that I was entering the room, told my father not to worry, I would soon change my mind and find something sensible to do. Many years later, the same woman shook my hand with genuine respect and congratulated me on my career. She had not read my books.

Why do we have this uncritical reverence for the published writer? Why does the simple fact of publication suddenly make a person, hitherto almost derided, now a proper object of our admiration, a repository of special and important knowledge about the human condition? And more interestingly, what effect does this shift from derision to reverence have on the author and his work, and on literary fiction in general?

Every year, I teach creative writing to just a couple of students. These are people in their mid-twenties in a British graduate program who come to me in Italy as part of an exchange. The prospect of publication, the urgent need, as they see it, to publish as soon as possible, colors everything they do. Often they will drop an interesting line of exploration, something they have been working on, because they feel compelled to produce something that looks more "publishable," which is to say, commercial. It will be hard for those who have never suffered this obsession to appreciate how all-conditioning and all-consuming it can be. These ambitious young people set deadlines for themselves. When the deadlines aren't met, their self-esteem plummets; a growing bitterness with the crassness of modern culture and the mercenary nature, as they perceive it, of publishers and editors barely disguises a crushing sense of personal failure.

But we're all aware of the woes of the wannabe. Less publicized is how the same mentality still feeds the world of fiction on the other side of the divide. For the day comes when wannabes, or at least a small percentage of them, are published. The letter, or phone call, or email arrives. In an instant life is changed. All at once you're being listened to with attention, you're on stage at literary festivals, you're under the spotlight at evening readings, being invited to be wise and solemn, to condemn this and applaud that, to speak of your next novel as a project of considerable significance, or indeed to pontificate on the future of the novel in general, or the future of civilization. Why not?

Neophytes are rarely unhappy with this. I have often been astonished how rapidly and ruthlessly young novelists, or simply first novelists, will sever themselves from the community of frustrated aspirants. After years of fearing oblivion, the published novelist now feels that success was inevitable, that at a very deep level *he always knew he was one of the elect* (something I remember V. S. Naipaul telling me at great length and with enviable conviction). They now live in a different dimension. Time is precious. Another book is required, because there is no point in establishing a reputation if it is not fed and exploited. Sure of their calling now, they buckle down to it.

All too soon they will become exactly what the public wants them to be: persons apart; producers of that special thing, literature; artists.

It alters everything. The dynamic in his marriage shifts. Or her marriage. An unpublished wife is one thing and a published wife quite another. The relationship with the children is conditioned by it. A new circle of friends is acquired. Yet as over time the author explores and grows into the position society so readily and generously grants to the artist, embracing or rejecting the opportunity to play the moralist, or alternatively the rebel—but the two so often coincide—to be constantly visible, or to retreat into a provocative invisibility, there nevertheless remains one thing he or she must never do. He must never acknowledge, or if he does so only ironically, as if really this were a joke, the fierce ambition that is driving this writing, and beneath that the presumption of an insuperable hierarchy between writer and reader, or simply writer and nonwriter, such that the former is infinitely more important, and indeed somehow more *real* than the latter.

Let's try to frame this more clearly. How many broad criteria are there for assessing or appraising another person? Not that many. Crudely we can think of them as good or evil, courageous or cowardly, belonging to our peer group or not belonging, talented or untalented, winners or losers. Naturally each of these criteria has its nuances and subsets, but basically, I think, that is it. And if I were asked which criterion is considered most important today, I would have to say the last. What matters is winning, sales, celebrity, world domination. Yet this must never be acknowledged as the principal value. So one wins while apparently championing other virtues and talking about quite other matters. In *Joseph Anton* Rushdie understandably raises the banner of freedom of speech—How is it fair, he asks at one point, that Margaret Thatcher is free to arrange a book presentation when I, because of the security costs, am not? This is not necessarily hypocrisy. One can care a great deal about this or that issue, or art form, or aesthetic, while beneath what still matters most is winning.

You can get interesting insights into this by opening up author websites, especially those of the less celebrated authors who maintain their sites themselves. Almost the first thing in front of you is a prize, an indication of success. "Born in Dublin in 1969, I am an award-winning writer" is the opening announcement from Emma Donoghue, author of the highly successful *Room*. Arnon Grunberg, arguably Holland's most successful living novelist, has a map of the world on which only those countries that have published his work are named. But they are many. Click on Egypt, Estonia, Japan and you can see what he has published there. Grunberg blogs in English and is clearly eager to have a world audience. So am I, for that matter. What is success without a world audience these days?

The question remains, why do people have such a high regard for authors, even when they don't read? Why do they flock to literary festivals, while sales of books fall? Perhaps it is simply because reverence and admiration are attractive emotions; we love to feel them, but in an agnostic world of ruthless individualism it gets harder and harder to find people you can bow down to without feeling a little silly. Politicians and military men no longer fit the bill. Sportsmen are just too lightweight, their careers so short-lived. In this sense it is a relief for the reader and even the nonreader to have a literary hero, at once talented and noble, perhaps even longsuffering, somebody who doesn't seem chiefly concerned with being more successful than we are. Alice Munro, with her endless, quietly sad accounts of people who fail to achieve their goals, gets it just right here: exploring that sense of failure so many feel in a competitive world, she wins the biggest prize of all.

DOES MONEY MAKE US WRITE BETTER?

LET'S TALK ABOUT money. In his history of world art, E. H. Gombrich mentions a Renaissance artist whose uneven work was a puzzle, until art historians discovered some of his accounts and compared incomes with images: paid less he worked carelessly; well-remunerated he excelled. So, given the falling income of writers over recent years— one thinks of the sharp drop in payments for freelance journalism and again in advances for most novelists, partly to do with a stagnant market for books, partly to do with the liveliness and piracy of the Internet—are we to expect a corresponding falling off in the quality of what we read? Can the connection really be that simple? On the other hand, can any craft possibly be immune from a relationship with money?

Asked to write blogs for other sites, some with much larger audiences, I chose to stay with *The New York Review of Books*, partly out of an old loyalty and partly because they pay me better. Would I write worse if I wrote for a more popular site for less money? Or would I write better because I was excited by the larger number of people following the site? And would this larger public then lead to my making more money some other way, say, when I sold a book to an American publisher? And if that book did make more money further down the line, having used the blog as a loss leader, does that mean the next book would be better written? Or do I always write the same way regardless of payment, so that these monetary transactions and the decisions that go with them affect my bank balance and anxiety levels, but not the quality of what I do?

Let's try to get some sense of this. When they are starting out, writers rarely make anything at all. I wrote seven novels over a period of six years before one was accepted for publication. Rejected by some twenty publishers, that seventh eventually earned me an advance of £1,000 for world rights. Evidently, I wasn't working for money. What then? Pleasure? I don't think so; I remember I was on the point of giving up when that book was accepted. I'd had enough. However much I enjoyed trying to get the world into words, the rejections were disheartening; and the writing habit was keeping me from a "proper" career elsewhere.

I was writing, I think, in my early twenties, to prove to myself that I could write, that I could become part of the community of writers, and it seemed to me I could not myself be the final judge of that. To prove I could write, that I could put together in words an interesting take on experience, I needed the confirmation of a publisher's willingness to invest in me, and I needed readers, hopefully serious readers, and critics. For me, that is, a writer was not just someone who writes, but someone who publishes and is read, and, yes, praised. Why I had set my heart on becoming that person remains unclear.

Today, of course, aspiring writers go to creative writing programs and so already have feedback from professionals. Many of them will self-publish short stories online and receive comments from unknown readers through the web. Yet I notice on the few occasions when I have taught creative writing courses that this encouragement, professional or otherwise, is never enough. Students are glad to hear that I think they can write, but they need, as I once needed, the confirmation of a publishing contract, which involves money. Not that they're calculating *how much* money, not at this point. They're thinking of a token of recognition—they want to exist, as writers.

Yet as soon as one has left the starting line, money matters. Of course it's partly a question of making ends meet; but there must be few novelists who believe they will live entirely from their writing as soon as a first novel is published. No, the money is important aside from a question of need because it indicates how much publishers are planning to invest in you, how much recognition they will afford you, how much they will push your book, getting you that attention you crave, and of course the level of the advance will tell you where you stand in relation to other authors. If the self-esteem that comes with "being a writer" can only be conferred when a publisher is willing to invest, it follows that the more they invest the more self-esteem they afford.

Is this a healthy state of affairs? Clearly we are far away from the minor Renaissance painter who coolly calibrates his efforts in relation to price, unflustered by concerns about his self-image or reputation in centuries to come. In his masterpiece *Jakob von Gunten*, Robert Walser has his young alter ego commiserate with his artist brother and question how a person can ever be at ease if his or her mental well-being depends on the critical judgment of others.

Paradoxically, then, almost the worst thing that can happen to writers, at least if it's the quality of their work we're thinking about, is to receive, immediately, all the money and recognition they want. At this point all other work, all other sane and sensible economic relation to society, is rapidly dropped and the said author now absolutely reliant on the world's response to his or her books, and at the same time most likely surrounded by people who will be building their own careers on his or her triumphant success, all eager to reinforce intimations of grandeur. An older person, long familiar with the utter capriciousness of the world's response to art, might deal with such an enviable situation with aplomb. For most of us it would be hard not to grow presumptuous and self-satisfied, or alternatively (but perhaps simultaneously) over-anxious to satisfy the expectations implied by six-figure payments. An interesting project, if any academic has the stomach to face the flak, would be to analyze the quality of the work of those young literary authors paid extravagant advances in the 1980s and 1990s; did their writing and flair, so far as these things can be judged, fall off along with the cash? For how long did the critical world remain in denial that their new darling was not producing the goods? Celebrity almost always outlives performance.

But if too much money can be damaging, dribs and drabs are not going to get the best out of a writer either. Our persistent romantic desire that the author, or at least his or her work, be somehow detached from the practicalities of money, together with the piety that insists that novels and poems be analyzed quite separately from the lives of their creators, has meant that there have been very few studies of the relationship between a writer's work and income. Randall Jarrell's 1965 introduction to Christina Stead's masterpiece, *The Man Who Loved Children* (1940), is a rare exception; seeking to recover Stead's writing for a new generation, Jarrell suggested that the Australian writer's failure to find a regular publisher—which he ascribed partly to her writing such wonderfully different novels, partly to her political position, and partly to her moving around so much from one country to another—eventually had a detrimental effect on her writing. Despite having written a dozen highly-praised novels, she had no community of reference, no group of critics who felt obliged to track her development from one work to the next, and as a result poor sales, to the point that she was eventually obliged to take in typing work to survive. Her profound sense of frustration and disillusionment began to color the writing itself, making it shriller and more self-indulgent, something Jarrell feels would not have happened had her publishing circumstances been different.

The important idea here, it seems to me, is that of a community of reference. Writers can deal with a modest income if they feel they are writing toward a body of readers who are aware of their work and buy enough of it to keep the publisher happy. But the nature of contemporary globalization, with its tendency to unify markets for literature, is such that local literary communities are beginning to weaken, while the divide between those selling vast quantities of books worldwide and those selling very few and mainly on home territory is growing all the time.

It would be intriguing here to run a comparison of the incomes and work of writers like U. R. Ananthamurthy, an Indian who has continued to write in his native Kannada language and whose translated fiction, when you can get hold of it, has all the difficulty and rewards of the genuinely exotic, and the far more familiar Indians writing in English (Salman Rushdie, Vikram Seth, and others) who have used their energy and imagination to present a version of India to the West where exoticism is at once emphasized and made easy. Ananthamurthy, in his eighties, has worked steadily and convincingly for decades, presumably on a fairly modest income; those more celebrated names, working in the glamour of huge advances and writing to the whole world rather than any particular community, find themselves constantly obliged to risk burnout in novels whose towering ambition might somehow justify their global reputation.

But for every Ananthamurthy there will be scores of local writers who did not find sufficient income to continue; for every Rushdie there will be hundreds whose reputation never reached that giddy orbit where a certain kind of literature can survive without the sustenance of a particular community of readers.

FEAR AND COURAGE

IS THE NOVEL a space of intense engagement with the world, of risk and adventure? Or is it a place of refuge, of hanging back from life? The answer will be all too easy if we are living in a country that does not allow certain stories to be told. For Solzhenitsyn writing novels was indeed a serious risk. But in the West?

I want to toss out a provocation: that in the world of literature there is a predominance of people whose approach to life is structured around issues of fear and courage and who find it difficult to establish a stable position in relation to those values. Not that they are necessarily more fearful than others, but that a sense of themselves as fearful or courageous is crucial for them and will be decisive in the structuring of both the content and style of their work.

That certain vocations attract a particular character type is evident enough. At the university where I work in Milan, we have two graduate programs for language students, one in interpreting and one in translation. With some exceptions the difference in attitude and character between members of the two groups is evident. The students who come to translation are not looking to be out there in the fray of the conference, under the spotlights; they like the withdrawn, intellectual aspect of translation. Often their problem as they begin their careers is not so much the work itself, but the self-marketing required to find the work.

It's also hardly revolutionary to suggest that literature can be seen simultaneously as an adventure and a refuge. Per Petterson's novels often feature a conflicted, anxious, but would-be courageous character surrounded by reckless friends and enemies. In *To Siberia* the young female protagonist is excited by images of Siberia she finds in a children's book and dreams of one day going there. Frightened of developments around her—the novel is set in wartime Denmark—she seeks comfort in reading, in fantasizing future adventures, but twice loses her source of books, once when a rich friend who has a library of her own suddenly dies, and once when a lesbian librarian makes aggressive advances at her. The virtual adventure and escape of reading is threatened by real adventure and calamity.

Throughout Petterson's work the main characters devote a great deal of time to practical tasks that will protect them from all kinds of dangers, or just the weather. They build huts and fires with immense care, because life is perilous, exciting, frightening. In the novel *It's Fine By Me*, a bildungsroman about a young Norwegian who looks for a way out of his depressing family situation in a life of writing, Petterson makes explicit that, as he sees it, the craft of writing, of carefully reconstructing life's precariousness in sentences as solid and unassuming as bricks, is itself a way of building shelter: for those who see danger everywhere, literature is a place of safety.

We could equally well look at a classic like *A Portrait of the Artist as a Young Man*. Stephen is constantly frightened. The first time his name is used, his mother is demanding an apology. Rather than confronting her, he hides under the table. His aunt threatens to pull out his eyes if he doesn't apologize. A page later he is frightened by the hurly burly of a rugby game. Pretending to participate because afraid of criticism, he actually hides on the edge of his line. The first time we see Stephen happy and relaxed, it is on his own in the sick bay where he is no longer obliged to engage in life in any way. Here for the first time we see him quoting lines of poetry, fantasizing, imagining, escaping, and in particular turning an imagined funeral into something beautiful, through words:

Two to sing and two to pray
And two to carry my soul away.
    How beautiful and sad that was! How beautiful the words were...

Terrified of the quarrel at Christmas lunch between the nationalist Mr. Casey and the fanatically Catholic Aunt Dante, Stephen focuses on the way the antagonists speak, the words they use, which allows him to keep out of the firing line, and creates an illusion of comfortable distance. Wishing to be a bold adolescent he goes to a prostitute; terrified by a Jesuit sermon on hell, he tries to be chaste and good. Eventually, courageously resisting all claims on his loyalty, he turns to art, claiming that the artist is by vocation beyond and above the factions. All the same he needs to justify himself by imagining that his work will courageously "forge the uncreated consciousness" of his race; disengaging with all parties he will single-handedly, from the safe distance of other countries, change Ireland. He claims. The decision to move to writing can thus be conceived as courageous on the one hand, or motivated by fear of succumbing to forces that terrify him on the other; his writing is a space of refuge, but he insists that it is engaged in changing the world.

Or what about the curious case of Thomas Hardy's first, unpublished novel? Having courageously left his village home to train as an architect in London, Hardy suddenly retreats to mother in Dorset-shire, pleading fatigue and illness (we have no record of any symptoms) and in 1867, aged twenty-seven, writes *The Poor Man and the Lady*, whose main character Will Strong, a bold Hardy alter ego, courts a rich man's daughter, is chased away by the family, and launches himself pugnaciously into politics. Hardy described the book as a "dramatic satire of the squirearchy...the tendency of the writing being socialistic, not to say revolutionary."

There are various accounts about why the novel was never published, but as Hardy has it, publication was offered, but the publisher's reader, the novelist George Meredith, warned him that the content was explosive and could damage his career. So, afraid of consequences, he withdrew it. Courage dominates in the story of the strong-willed Will Strong, but not in Hardy's dealings with his publishers; he is courageous only in so far as he supposes the work will not intersect with reality. He then set about writing the entirely innocuous comedy *Desperate Remedies* (the title says it all). Later in his career Hardy did take on Victorian morals very courageously in *Tess of the D'Urbervilles* and *Jude the Obscure*, but was so harrowed by the aggressive reviews he received that he chose to stop writing fiction and turned to the much safer production of poetry. "No more novel-writing for me," he remarked. "A man must be a fool to deliberately stand up to be shot at."

One could name any number of novels in which the tension between a desire for and fear of intense experience is played out in all kinds of ways: J. M. Coetzee's *Youth* and Damon Galgut's *The Good Doctor* are two contemporary novels that immediately come to mind; Coetzee's characters are often eager to be tested by life, but at the same time afraid that they will be caught out, found to be lacking in courage. Peter Stamm's novels (*Unformed Landscape*, *On a Day Like This*, and *Seven Years*) suggest how the need to create narratives for our lives forces us toward moments of risk and engage-ment, while fear of those moments may lead us to fantasize a self narrative rather than really act, or alternatively to become hyper-rational and cautious in our decision making. These antithetical en-ergies, toward and away from adventure, are mirrored in the writing itself as Stamm sets the reader up for melodrama, then seems to do everything to avoid or postpone it, as if, like his characters, he would much prefer to plod quietly along with life's routine, but knows that sooner or later, alas, a writer has to deliver the goods.

So much, then, for a fairly common theme in literature. It's under-standable that those sitting comfortably at a dull desk to imagine life at its most intense might be conflicted over questions of courage and fear. It's also more than likely that this divided state of mind is shared by a certain kind of reader, who, while taking a little time out from life's turmoil, nevertheless likes to feel that he or she is reading coura-geous books.

The result is a rhetoric that tends to flatter literature, with every-body overeager to insist on its liveliness and import. "The novel is the one bright book of life," D. H. Lawrence tells us. "Books are not life," he immediately goes on to regret. "They are only tremulations on the ether. But the novel as a tremulation can make the whole man alive tremble." Lawrence, it's worth remembering, grew up in the shadow of violent parental struggles and would always pride himself on his readiness for a fight, regretting in one letter that he was too ill "to slap Frieda [his wife] in the eye, in the proper marital fashion," but "re-duced to vituperation." Frieda, it has to be said, gave as good as she got. In any event words just weren't as satisfying as blows, though Lawrence did everything he could to make his writing feel like a fight: "whoever reads me will be in the thick of the scrimmage," he insisted.

In *How Fiction Works* James Wood tells us that the purpose of fic-tion is "to put life on the page" and insists that "readers go to fiction for life." Again there appears to be an anxiety that the business of literature might have more to do with withdrawal; in any event one can't help thinking that someone in search of life would more likely be flirting, traveling, or partying. How often on a Saturday evening in my university days would the call to life lift my head from my books and have me hurrying out into the street.

This desire to convince oneself that writing is at least as alive as life itself, was recently reflected by a *New York Times* report on brain-scan research that claims that as we read about action in novels the areas of the brain that would be responsible for such action in real life—those that respond to sound, smell, texture, movement, etc.—are activated by the words. "The brain, it seems," writes the journalist, "does not make much of a distinction between reading about an experience and encountering it in real life; in each case, the same neurological regions are stimulated."

What nonsense! As if reading about sex or violence in any way prepared us for the experience of its intensity. (In this regard I recall my adolescent daughter's recent terror on seeing our border collie go into violent death throes after having eaten some poison in the countryside. As the dog foamed at the mouth and twitched, Lucy was shivering, weeping, appalled. But day after day she reads gothic tales and watches hard-core horror movies with a half smile on her lips.)

The same *New York Times* article quotes Keith Oatley, a cognitive psychologist and, significantly, "a published novelist" who claims that

> reading produces a vivid simulation of reality, one that runs on minds of readers just as computer simulations run on computers.... Indeed, in one respect novels go beyond simulating reality to give readers an experience unavailable off the page: the opportunity to enter fully into other people's thoughts and feelings.

If Oatley genuinely believes this I suspect he is not a very good novel-ist, novels being largely about form and convention. Halfway through *Seven Years* Peter Stamm, who I believe is an excellent novelist, has his narrator describe his oddly quiet and passive mistress thus:

> My relationship with Ivona had been, from the start, nothing other than a story, a parallel world that obeyed my will, and where I could go wherever I wanted, and could leave when I'd had enough.

Nothing other than a story. How disappointing. How reassuring. The passage seems to be worded in such a way as to suggest the au-thor's own frustration with his quiet and safe profession. But a mis-tress is a mistress, and a novel a novel. To ask her or it to be more than that would be to ask the mistress to become a wife, and the novel a life. Which it can never be.

TO TELL AND NOT TO TELL

"HER HUSBAND was deeply hurt when she published her novel..."

"The author's father was disgusted by what he had written...

"His wife was furious..." etc.

Is information like this ever more than gossip? Can we learn anything about literature by reflecting on the responses of the writer's family and loved ones? What Christina Stead's partner thought about *Letty Fox: Her Luck*, for example, where the writer presented his daughter by a previous marriage as a promiscuous sexual opportunist. Or how Emma Hardy reacted when she saw her sexual problems discussed in the pages of *Jude the Obscure*. Or the embarrassment of Faulkner's parents when he published *Soldiers' Pay*.

"Serious" critics rarely venture into this territory. It is beneath their dignity. I mean academics: the book must be read on its own terms without the distractions of biography. Yet ordinary readers and some reviewers find it hard not to wonder about this tension in the writer's life and how it might relate to the work. The narrator of Philip Roth's *Deception*, himself called Philip Roth, tells his wife: "I write fiction and I'm told it's autobiography, I write autobiography and I'm told it's fiction, so since I'm so dim and they're so smart, let *them* decide what it is or it isn't." For Roth there were few taboos left to break at this point and any partner of his could consider herself well warned. With other writers much may be at stake.

"I could never have written a book like that," a friend and writer remarked to me of my first novel, "for fear of what my mother would say." "Parks's nearest and dearest," wrote the novelist Patrick Gale, reviewing another book of mine, "must await each of his publications with growing trepidation." For Gale, part of the experience of reading the novel was wondering about its genesis and consequences. The story on the page hints at a life story beyond.

The question is: Can a novel that will affect the author's closest relationships be written without any concern for the consequences? Will the story perhaps be "edited" to avoid the worst? Or is awareness of the possible reaction part of the energy feeding the book? Italo Svevo's *La Coscienza di Zeno* begins with a hilarious account of Zeno's attempts to stop smoking, always stymied by his decision to treat himself to *l'ultima sigaretta*, the last cigarette, usually one of the highest quality. Friends were aware this was largely autobiographical. The novel continues with Zeno's courting of three sisters; eventually rejected by the two prettiest, he marries the plain one. Again his wife would have been aware of elements from his own life. And now we have the story of a love affair, its various stages recounted in the most meticulous and again hilarious, all-too-convincing psychological detail. Finally, we proceed to chapters on Zeno's business life, which much resembles Svevo's own running of a paint company. Nevertheless the author's wife always stated with great serenity that she was sure her husband had never betrayed her, nor was she shaken in this belief by the fact that his last words, when pulled out of a car accident were, reputedly, "Give me *l'ultima sigaretta*."

So, was the introduction of the affair into the novel a kind of trial for her? She had to believe it was just made up. Or was there an agreement between them, explicit or otherwise, that whatever they knew would be kept to themselves, any truth in the matter forever denied? Did Svevo have to introduce the mistress because the shape of the novel required it? If so, wouldn't there be a certain anxiety that his wife wouldn't see it that way, and wouldn't that affect the way he wrote these chapters?

What I am suggesting is that in the genesis of a novel, or any work of literature, there will often be private tensions playing a part in the creative decisions made. If a reader becomes aware of these tensions, that awareness will inevitably alter the way the book is read. Some years ago, reading Joseph Frank's mammoth biography of Dostoevsky, comparing dates and details in footnotes, I realized to my astonishment that when the author was writing *Notes from Underground*, in which at one point the utterly disgraceful narrator scares the living daylights out of a young prostitute by foreseeing how she will die of tuberculosis in the brothel, Dostoevsky's own wife was dying of tuberculosis in the next room. While he imagined his character telling the girl she would still be submitting to her clients' clumsy caresses while coughing blood, he could hear his wife coughing blood on the other side of the wall. This biographical "story"— the circumstances in which Dostoevsky wrote the work—altered and intensified the novel's story for me, if only because the wife's illness and Dostoevsky's very difficult relationship with her (he had recently returned from a gambling spree and an affair with a younger woman) very likely had to do with the frighteningly negative energy coming off the page.

Might we then suppose that in creating a novel, an author is using many levels of address, ranging from utterances directed to those closest to the author, perhaps even in a sense exclusively to him or herself, and utterances addressed to everyone? So that certain aspects of a novel are, in fact, or are *also*, conversations overheard, and as such perhaps more intriguing than comprehensible? Is this what creates an element of enigma in many writers' narratives, a surplus of emotion that seems to go beyond the apparent content?

In any case, who is this "everyone" the author is addressing? Certainly not readers in the past, who are dead and cannot read his work. Perhaps not those in distant lands and cultures, or in a distant future, whose opinions and attitudes the author doesn't know and cannot easily relate to. "Everyone" in fact means the people the author assumes will be reading the book. "I've just done the last proofs of Lady C [*Lady Chatterley's Lover*]," D. H. Lawrence wrote in 1928. "I *hope* it'll make 'em howl—and let 'em do their paltry damnedest, after." In this case "them" was more or less everybody in the British establishment. *They* were the people Lawrence was addressing, not us, not the German or Italian publics, not a twenty-first-century student in Seoul writing a doctoral thesis on Lawrence. (An extraordinary number of doctoral theses on Lawrence have come out of South Korea.) Thus, we are *overhearing* Lawrence's argument with his English contemporaries, hence a little knowledge about them and him will give the experience of reading the novel more sense and depth.

Our "serious critics" have no problem with this; they acknowledge that context will be helpful in reading a book that comes from the past, or from another country. But isn't this absolutely analogous to taking an interest in the extent to which a book affects the author's more intimate relationships? Surely this was of more importance than his or her attitude toward the general public. After all, Lawrence frequently and blatantly put people he knew in his novels and seemed to relish the fallout. Joyce did the same.

Eugenio Montale, a poet who remained married while pursuing long affairs with other women, regretted the passing some five hundred years ago of the sonnet sequence convention which, as he saw it, had created a form that everybody could contribute to without the question of biography arising; indeed, what most attracts him to the *stilnovisti* of the thirteenth century—the Tuscan poets who preceded Dante—is the way their poems appear as a collective effort, such that any discussion of individual biographical events becomes meaningless. Clearly what Montale sought was the freedom, in his many poems addressed to women, either to invent or not to invent without having others pursue the matter. At the same time, the implication is that much artistic convention depends on a desire to find public expression for what must remain hidden in private, such that a married person writing of a lover can claim to do so, or maybe indeed truly do so, because such writing constitutes a beautiful convention to which he or she wishes to contribute, not because he or she has a lover and not because he or she likes to imagine having a lover without actually having one, something some spouses might in fact find more distasteful.

It would seem that fiction writing is trying to satisfy two needs that are at loggerheads: to tell and not to tell. The anthropologist Gregory Bateson, who wrote a great deal about how art is often a therapeutic corrective mechanism in society, suggested that any long-term intimate relationship depended on mutual respect of both partners for a taboo; it was precisely the agreed silence about core facts that allowed a relationship to become, as it were, chronic or, looking at it more positively, stable. If that is the case, the fascinating question about works of literature that risk arousing the hostility of the author's loved ones is: Does the energy and urgency of the story actually depend on the author's breaking or perhaps not quite breaking a taboo? Or rather, is the author finding in fiction a way to smuggle a message through the taboo, while leaving it officially intact? Ultimately one might see a great deal of literature as the happy byproduct of a disturbing communication problem.

STUPID QUESTIONS

WHY DO PEOPLE ask such stupid questions?

At a literary festival in Bordeaux I found myself being introduced to the French writer Frédéric Verger. I wasn't familiar with the name, and he explained that he had published just one novel, but that it had been shortlisted for this year's Prix Goncourt. Since he was evidently in his mid-fifties, I was surprised, and asked him how come he had started so late. He explained that he had tried novels in his early twenties, been rejected, spent much of his life teaching literature in high school and then decided to try again, this time with success. It was an unusual story. I asked him how his presentations were going at the festival and he said fine, except that at the end the public asked such dumb questions.

"Like?"

"Like why I've only written one novel when I'm fifty-four."

Most writers complain about the people who come to hear them talk. Or rather the questions they ask. We need the public, of course, to feel important, to have a reason for presenting our books. When the seats are all full we say it is a good audience, we're enthusiastic, especially if they show signs of participation when we read. If they laugh when they should, in particular. "But when it comes to questions, they always ask about your life," complains Caroline Lamarche. She is sitting next to me at a book signing. The French have what I am sure is a counterproductive policy of getting authors to sit for hours at a time at book stands in sweltering pavilions just in case someone should want to buy a book of theirs and have it autographed. This way we look like country folk who have brought their beans to market, undermining commercially useful myths of our charismatic and mysterious talent. Still, the scene does give me time to examine the covers of Lamarche's novels. They appear to be about love, sex, and violence. She seems an interesting lady and I would like to ask her a little about her life, but am afraid of seeming dumb.

In a car heading to the airport, I'm alone in the backseat while the two up front—one of the festival organizers and a fellow writer—chat away in French. I look up the writer's photo in the festival catalog and find his name, Louis Philippe Dalembert, he hails from Port-au-Prince. Then I see that his novel *Ballade d'un amour inachevé* "revisits the earthquakes of L'Aquila and Haiti, at both of which the author found himself involved." L'Aquila is in the Abruzzo region of Italy, my territory. I toss in a question in Italian and it turns out Dalembert speaks the language perfectly. His wife is from L'Aquila, mine from Pescara just down the road. He talks interestingly about being in the city the days after the quake, the question of whether to write about it and if so, whether a memoir or a novel. In fact it was while he was mulling this over that he went back to Haiti for a visit and got caught up in the quake there. I ask him how his presentation went. "Fine, but for the stupid questions afterwards," he says.

Enough. It's time to wonder whether these people who come to see us talk about our books are really asking dumb questions, or the wrong questions. Why are writers so determined to focus exclusively on their novels, as if there were no continuity between writing and life?

One of the problems is how difficult it is to talk usefully and entertainingly about books in these circumstances. One arrives in a tent with a hundred-odd seats, of which half are occupied. A presenter who may or may not have really read your book offers a potted version of your life that mainly amounts to age, bibliography, and accolades. The novel you are presenting is sketched out: a few items of plot, the suggestion of some kind of theme or message. Listening to this, you are overwhelmed by the enormous gap between the density and complexity, the sheer volume of what you have written and this drastic reduction.

Meantime, among the audience, a small group have already read the book, so anything they hear about it is infinitely less than what they already know. Another group have never read anything you've written, so they are hardly the wiser from these few formulaic crumbs. Those who've read other books of yours but not this one will be trying to fit what's being said with what they've read, which, if you write very similar novels, may be easy enough, and if you write drastically different ones, well nigh impossible. In my case the present novel is set at a meditation retreat, but they may have read the one featuring kayaking in the alps, or a coach trip to take a petition to the European Parliament.

The only sensible approach would be to read a bit of the book itself. An author's voice, posture, manner, body language, as they read the opening paragraphs of a story, their coldness or warmness, shyness or wryness, heat or humor, can give a powerful impression. Unfortunately, many festivals in Europe discourage reading. They're afraid you'll go on forever and bore them to tears. At most the person presenting you will read out a paragraph or two. As he does so you sit there bewildered that he should choose this of all paragraphs, amazed that he could get the tone of the work so wrong. He doesn't hear it at all. Convinced you will be underestimated and misunderstood, you launch into an long "explanation" of your book, the initial idea, the models that inspired you, the particular spin you were looking for, but even as you do so you are aware that at some deep level, none of this is true. The whole business was all so much more elusive and complicated. The public watch pokerfaced, whether bored or sympathetic you don't know. Finally the presenter says it's time to ask if anyone has any questions. A hand is raised: "Have you ever been to a Buddhist retreat yourself?" an elderly woman asks. "If so, why and would you recommend it?"

So, is this, or is this not a stupid question?

Most of the people who attend these events are regular readers. And of course they have come to events before. They are not fools. They have long since understood that almost nothing of interest can really be said about books at an event. They know that a novel is too sprawling and too complicated and the meshing of minds that occurs when novelist and reader meet on the page too intimate and elusive a process really to be tackled in forty public minutes with iffy microphones and occasional entries and departures.

So what did they come here for? Enjoying books, reading frequently, the experience leaves them curious perhaps. They want to understand why books make such a deep impression on them. Perhaps they feel there is a surplus of meaning, beyond the novel's obvious excitements that they haven't been able to articulate. Something has come across to them that is not to be isolated in anything said on the page. In short, there is a mystery they would like to understand and that mystery is you. Or they construe it as you. They feel if they knew more about you, about writers in general, it might put their minds to rest as to the experience of reading. Perhaps.

For your part you know perfectly well that there is an absolute continuity between this book and your life. You will talk about the book as if you were in control of its creation, and perhaps you are to a degree, but behind and before that is a vast hinterland of experience and events over which you had no control. Only you could have written this particular book, not because you are better or more imaginative than anyone else, but because you are you. So much is said about the unlimited nature of the imagination, but actually the simple truth is that only DeLillo can imagine what DeLillo imagines and he could never imagine what Roth imagines, nor quite likely would he want to. The limit of this unlimited imagination is you. This book is your book. Who could it come from but you?

"Do you think your move to Italy altered the way you think and write?"

"Has it been useful for you as an author to translate as well?"

"Does your wife read your books and if so what does she think of them?"

None of these questions are directly addressed to the novel you are presenting. Yet one has to grant that if one only knew the answers, something would be learned. The public are firing shots in the dark; they are groping for some kind of connection between the figure on the stage and the particular atmosphere of the novels they have read. A disturbing atmosphere. A heartening atmosphere. Or disturbing *and* heartening, and funny *and* decidedly unfunny. Why so? Who are you, to be producing this stuff? That's what they're asking. The irony perhaps is that what's mysterious to them is even more mysterious to you. Yet even as you try and inevitably fail to answer their questions you are probably telling them more, in your perplexity and frustration, or your wryness and charm, than you ever could have by explaining your book.

THE CHATTERING MIND

"WHO IS THE most memorable character in the novels of the twentieth century?"

It's a typical radio ploy to fill some mental space on a Saturday morning. Dutifully, people phone in. Studio guests discuss their choices. The obvious: Leopold Bloom, Gatsby. The wry: Jeeves, Sir Peter Wimsey. To select Proust's unnamed narrator of *In Search of Lost Time* indicates a certain sophistication. Somebody, not a child, proposes Harry Potter. Then Miss Marple, Svevo's Zeno, James Bond, Gustav von Aschenbach, Richard Hannay. People are telling us about themselves of course. They want to talk about themselves. There's no question of our establishing whether Frodo Baggins is really more influential than José Arcadio Buendía or Bellow's Herzog. But Sherlock Holmes can be safely ruled out because he first appears in the nineteenth century and Lisbeth Salander because she doesn't turn up until 2005.

I can't be bothered to think of a name myself. I resist these games—the most this, the best that. Surely these characters are all actors in a grand cast; they all have their roles in the larger drama of the collective psyche. But now suddenly it occurs to me that by far the main protagonist of twentieth-century literature must be the chattering mind, which usually means the mind that can't make up its mind, the mind postponing action in indecision and, if we're lucky, poetry.

There were plenty of forewarnings. Hamlet is the most notable. To take action would be to confirm his identity as his father's son, his father's avenger, but Hamlet thinks too precisely on the event, he's too smart, and so fails to become anyone at all, either his father's son or Ophelia's husband. He suffers for that failure and spins out unhappy procrastination in fine poetry. In a comic vein, Tristram Shandy is another forerunner, too aware of his narrative performance to narrate anything coherent, let alone act. Both Hamlet and Tristram are characters who didn't reach the height of their popularity until the twentieth century. We had become like them.

Prone to qualification, self-contradiction, interminable complication, this new kind of character finds his most sinister early manifestation in the narrator of Dostoevsky's *Notes from Underground*. "I am a wicked man," this nameless individual introduces himself, then reflects "but as a matter of fact, I was never able to become wicked. I never managed to become anything: neither wicked nor good, neither a scoundrel nor an honest man, neither a hero nor an insect." Again, the reason for this indeterminacy is an excess of intellectual activity; so the cause for failure is also a source of self-esteem: "An intelligent man of the nineteenth century," Dostoevsky's narrator tells us, with a mixture of complacency and despair, "must be and is morally obliged to be primarily a characterless being; and a man of character, an active figure—primarily a limited being." Seeing the pros and cons of every possible move, this modern man is paralyzed, half envying those less intelligent than himself who throw themselves instinctively into the fray: "[The man of action] is stupid, I won't argue with you about that, but perhaps a normal man ought to be stupid." And the voice is actually pleased with this formulation. It's great to feel superior to those happier than oneself.

In the twentieth century this monstrously heightened conscious-ness meshes with the swelling background noise of modern life, and we have the full-blown performing mind of modernist literature. It starts perhaps in that room where the women come and go, talking of Michelangelo. Soon Leopold Bloom is diffusing his anxiety about Molly's betrayal in the shop signs and newspaper advertisements of Dublin. In Mrs. Dalloway's London, people muddle thoughts of their private lives with airborne advertisements for toffee, striking clocks, sandwich men, omnibuses, chauffeur-driven celebrities.

Looking back, what surprises us is how enthusiastically the liter-ary world welcomed this new hero. Prufrock's mind might be trapped, inept, and miserable, but it is wonderfully poetic. I'll never forget how my high-school teacher gushed. Bloom may be incapable of im-posing any direction on his marriage, drifting between fantasy and frustration as his wife prepares to betray, and Stephen Dedalus may be marooned in an impossible relationship with his father and jobs that give him no satisfaction, yet *Ulysses* is a celebration of the inex-haustible fertility of their minds as they move through the commer-cial flotsam and jetsam of Dublin against the vast backdrop of world literature and myth. It's all quite reassuring, even self-congratulatory. What wonderful minds we have, even though they don't seem to get us anywhere, or make us happy.

Virginia Woolf sounds darker notes, warning us that the mind risks being submerged by the urgent blather of modern life; yet in the end even the crazy, shell-shocked Septimus Warren Smith gives us para-graph after paragraph of poetic prose before he throws himself to his death from a high window, something that Clarissa Dalloway will think of as an act of impulsive generosity. It's as if the stream of con-sciousness had been invented to allow the pain of a mind whose chat-ter is out of control to be transformed into a strange new beauty, which then encompasses the one action available to the stalled self: suicide.

The way this aesthetic consolation is constructed shifts constantly through the century. Faulkner has no time for the easy lyricism of the mind adrift on the ebb and flow of urban trivia. Now the unending voice revolves obsessively around the traumas that block any positive forward movement: past wrongs, sexual violence and betrayal, incest, the disgrace of institutionalized discrimination. Still, there is grandeur in the sheer scale and awfulness of the mind's shipwreck, individual and collective. Slowly you get the feeling that only mental suffering and impasse confer dignity and nobility. Our twentieth-century author is simply not interested in a mind that does not suffer, usually in extended syntax, and not interested in dramatizing the traumatic event itself, only the blocked and suffering consciousness that broods on it afterward.

Beckett resists and confirms the formula. He understands its perversity: pleasure taken in the performance of unhappiness: "Can there be misery loftier than mine?" he has the aptly named Hamm remark in the first moments of *Endgame*. Beckett exposes the spiral whereby the more the mind circles around its impasse, taking pride in its resources of observation, the deeper the impasse becomes, the sharper the pain, the greater the need to find a shred of self-respect in the ability at least to describe one's downfall. And so on. But understanding the trap, and the perversity of the consolation that confirms the trap, doesn't mean you've found a way out of it; to have seen through literary consolation is just another source of consolation: at least I've understood and brilliantly dramatized the futility of my brilliant exploration of my utter impotence.

Michel Butor, Nathalie Sarraute, Alain Robbe-Grillet, Thomas Bernhard, Philip Roth, John Updike, David Foster Wallace, James Kelman, Alison Kennedy, Will Self, Sandro Veronesi, and scores upon scores of others all find new ways of exasperating and savoring this mental chatter: minds crawling through mud in the dark, minds trapped in lattices of light and shade, minds dividing into many voices, minds talking to themselves in second person, minds enthralled in sexual obsession, minds inflaming themselves with every kind of intoxicant, minds searching for oblivion, but not finding it, fearing they may not find it even in death.

Not long after that Saturday-morning radio show I sat in a meditation retreat and heard a speaker expound the Buddha's well-known reflection on the so-called "second arrow." A student had come to him with questions about pain, meditation, suffering. The Buddha replied with a question of his own: "When someone is struck by an arrow, is it painful?" "Yes," said the student. Then another question: "When this someone is struck by a second arrow, is it painful?" "Of course it is," said the student. Then the Buddha said, "There is nothing you can do about the first arrow. You are bound to encounter pain. However the second arrow is your choice. You can choose to decline the second arrow."

Sitting for ten days on a cushion, eyes closed, cross-legged, seeking to empty your mind of words, it's all too evident how obsessively the mind seeks to construct self-narrative, how ready it is to take interest in its own pain, to congratulate itself on the fertility of its reflection. That chattersome voice will even be pleased with its progressively more elaborate analyses of how difficult it is to quiet the mind and empty it of the very reflections it is making. But alas, you cannot sit cross-legged without pain unless you learn to relax your body very deeply. And, as neuroscience has recently confirmed, when the mind churns words, the body tenses. As if in a laboratory, one is obliged to experiment with the perils and pleasures of what the Buddha called the second arrow, the mind bringing energy to its own pain.

But you can also choose not to go that way. You can decide that your mental chatter is not after all so damn interesting; the second arrow can be declined. How else would these people around you have learned to sit so still, for so long and in such serenity? Imagine Dostoevsky's man in *Notes from Underground*, or Beckett's Unnameable, or Thomas Bernhard's narrator in *The Loser* at a meditation retreat, learning to be silent, learning to sit still, learning to put to rest the treadmill of reflection.

Or again, imagine if the literary folk suddenly tired of it all, realized how unhelpful it all was; if the critics and academics wearied of untangling torment for a living (I see you haven't got any better, Beckett's old analyst responded after the author sent him a copy of *Watt*). Imagine if the publishers—let's call them the Second Arrow Publishing Corporation—informed all their great authors, all the masters of the mercilessly talkative consciousness, that they are winding up their affairs; they have seen the light, they will no longer publish elaborations of tortured consciousness, lost love, frustrated ambition, however ingenious or witty. Imagine! All the great sufferers saved by Buddhism, declining the second arrow: quietness where there was Roth, serenity where there was McCarthy, well-being where there was David Foster Wallace.

Do we want that?

I suspect not. I suspect our destiny is to pursue our literary sickness for years to come. It is hard not to congratulate oneself on the quality of one's unhappiness. "Every word," Beckett told us, "is an unnecessary stain on silence," then began:

Where now? Who now? When now? Unquestioning. I, say I. Unbelieving. Questions, hypotheses, call them that. Keep going, going on, call that going, call that on.

TRAPPED INSIDE THE NOVEL

I WONDER HOW many people share the experience described by David Shields in *Reality Hunger*, of tackling some large novel, a work essentially conventional in its structure and brand of realism, that weaves together the lives of its characters over a number of years, and simply feeling that the whole exercise has become irrelevant. Shields doesn't present his remarks as a criticism of writers—the name he mentions is Jonathan Franzen—pursuing the tradition of the long realistic novel. Rather, he suggests it is a change in himself, something he believes has been brought about by the utterly changed nature of contemporary life. He considers the variety of electronic media—the proliferation and abbreviation of all forms of messages, the circumstances created by the evermore rapid transit and greater abundance of information, the emergence of a powerful virtual world that becomes more real to us all the time—and he concludes that given this way of life, it is hard for the traditional kind of novel to hold our attention.

I share Shields's changing reaction to traditional novels. More and more I wonder if it is possible for a novel not to give me the immediate impression of being manipulated toward goals that are predictable and unquestioned: the dilemma, the dramatic crisis, the pathos, the wise sadness, and in general a suffering made bearable, or even noble through aesthetic form, fine prose, and the conviction that one has lived through something important. But to go from that to fragmented, rapidly intercut chunks of "reality," however powerfully they may evoke certain aspects of contemporary living, doesn't work for me, nor do I entirely agree with Shields' analysis, however strongly and passionately he makes his case.

First of all, it is clear that many people who are entirely at home with their iPhones and iPads, music clapped to their ears and text messages vibrating in their pockets, still very much enjoy the traditional novel—regardless of whether it offers an account of life that corresponds to theirs. Otherwise how to explain the vast numbers of readers picking up the work of a Hilary Mantel, a Richard Ford, or, on the more popular side, a Stieg Larsson or an E. L. James? If the form is losing its seduction for some, it is clearly alive and well for many. Indeed, its very distance, in most cases, from the texture of modern life, the impression it can give of shape, continuity, and hence meaning, may be its most reassuring and attractive aspect. The growing popularity of historical novels would tend to confirm this. Such works as *Wolf Hall*, this year's Man Booker winner *The Luminaries* (both more than six hundred pages), and the prize's "runner-up," Jim Crace's *Harvest*, or again the much-praised *Traveler of the Century* by Spanish novelist Andrés Neuman, all suggest in different ways that, despite its enigmas, we know more or less what a life is or should be, we can follow its trajectories, we can put the past in relation to the present.

This is exactly where my dissatisfaction with the form begins. Over recent years I have preferred the works of writers, many long dead, who seemed to share my anxiety that the traditional form was scandalously overconfident: Beckett's novels, Thomas Bernhard's, more recently the strange amalgamation that is Lydia Davis's lifelong collection of short *stories*, if stories really is the right word for them. Even so, this kind of writing, and with it the whole postmodern adventure, seems to derive its energy by gauging its distance from the traditional novel, by expressing its disbelief and frustration with the form, and there is a limit to the pleasures, comedy, and wisdom of negative energy and deconstruction. One risks ending up like the goat in Beckett's *Watt*, who, chained to a post, has wrenched the post from the ground, but has no idea where to go and is hampered by the chain still fastened round his neck and by the post that continues to clatter wherever he turns. The pathos of failing to achieve meaning replaces the more immediate pathos that clings in the traditional narrative to the characters' meaningful lives. But Beckett's fiction, however wonderful, is the novel as noble dead end, a heroic bivouac on the edge of a civilization in denial.

My problem with the grand traditional novel—or rather traditional narrative in general, short stories included—is the vision of character, the constant reinforcement of a fictional selfhood that accumulates meaning through suffering and the overcoming of suffering. At once a palace built of words and a trajectory propelled by syntax, the self connects effortlessly with the past and launches bravely into the future. Challenged, perhaps thwarted by circumstance, it nevertheless survives, with its harvest of bittersweet consolation, and newly acquired knowledge.

I'm being reductive. The variety of stories told in the novel is indeed remarkable, but the tendency to reinforce in the reader the habit of projecting his or her life as a meaningful story, a narrative that will very likely become a trap, leading to inevitable disappointment followed by the much-prized (and I suspect overrated) wisdom of maturity, is nigh on universal. Likewise, and intrinsic to this approach, is the invitation to shift our attention away from the moment, away from any real savoring of present experience, toward the past that brought us to this point and the future that will likely result. The present is allowed to have significance only in so far as it constitutes a position in a story line. Intellect, analysis, and calculation are privileged over sense and immediate perception; the whole mind is pushed toward the unceasing construction of meaning, of narrative intelligibility, of underlying structure, without which life is assumed to be unimaginable or unbearable.

It is a way of seeing that is bound to produce states of profound disappointment for those who subscribe to it. "Munro brilliantly tracks the lives of those who did not achieve what they expected to," exclaimed one British paper after the 2013 Nobel Prize was announced. It hardly seems a cause for congratulation if the Western mindset is constructed around first projecting extravagant ambitions, the infamous "dream," and then relying on authors like Alice Munro to offer consolation when it isn't achieved, or alternatively seeks to enjoy success vicariously by reading celebrity biographies, another increasingly popular genre. In this regard, one can even see the consolations of literature as one of the forces sustaining a destructive cultural pattern. We are so pleased with our ability to describe and savor our unhappiness, it hardly seems important to find a different way of going about things.

What I don't understand is whether this kind of narrative strategy is a natural consequence of choosing the novel form, or simply the default setting of fiction in our culture. Beckett famously felt that the problems of literary fiction were inherent in language itself, in its overconfident, unquestioning forward motion, and that the only response possible was, as it were, to write against *language*, to expose it, have it trip itself up. In a much-quoted letter written in 1937, he even imagined a time when language itself might be dissolved or eliminated:

It is indeed becoming more and more difficult, even senseless, for me to write an official English. And more and more my own language appears to me like a veil that must be torn apart in order to get at the things (or the Nothingness) behind it. Grammar and Style. To me they seem to have become as irrelevant as a Victorian bathing suit or the imperturbability of a true gentleman. A mask. Let us hope the time will come...when language is most efficiently used where it is being most efficiently misused. As we cannot eliminate language all at once, we should at least leave nothing undone that might contribute to its falling into disrepute. To bore one hole after another in it, until what lurks behind it—be it something or nothing—begins to seep through; I cannot imagine a higher goal for a writer today.

A few years ago, Colm Tóibín—at present one of the finest masters of the traditional narrative form, the dying fall, the sad accumulation of pathos and wisdom—observed that Beckett himself was second to none when it came to manipulating grammar and style, as if that constituted a contradiction. Not at all: the problem lies exactly in feeling that one's skills are only suitable for a project that no longer makes sense. So many writers are now able to produce passable imitations of our much-celebrated nineteenth-century novels (again *The Luminaries* is a case in point). Their very facility becomes an obstacle to exploring some more satisfactory form.

So, is there a way forward in words that could express a quite different vision of self and narrative? In my own small way I tried to do this in my recent novel *Sex is Forbidden*, where a young woman in a Buddhist meditation center is seeking to move away from mental habits—ambition, regret, unhappy love—which have entrapped and humiliated her. I don't think I succeeded. Buddhism, as a set of teachings and practices that invite the dissipation of the "fiction" of self and a quite different idea of social involvement and personal trajectory, became in the end simply a stark contrast that exposed the extent to which the girl was trapped in the Western obsession of creating one's own successful life story. Most readers, I'm sure, were eager for her to avoid the seductions of nirvana. More generally, the tale's literary nature, its very presentation of itself as a novel—perhaps I just mean my own ambitions—inevitably dragged it back toward the old familiar ploys, the little climaxes, the obligatory ironies. True, one could set them up and then retreat from them, prepare and not deliver, encourage the reader to see how wearisomely novels do go in a certain direction. But the whole endeavor was like sailing against a strong wind: however determinedly you point to the open sea, you are constantly blown back on the familiar coast. When the moment comes to discuss the blurb with the publisher, you know that you haven't done anything new.

To conclude: in 2011 I had occasion to visit an old university tutor, a rather severe and demanding professor, who nevertheless played a generous part in encouraging me to write. He read my first attempts at fiction and introduced me to writers who would later be important to me, most notably Henry Green. I had not seen him in thirty years. Long since retired, he was now restricted to a wheelchair and, with time on his hands, had been re-reading old favorites, all the great novels that had inspired a lifetime's career in reading, writing, teaching. We talked about Faulkner, Fitzgerald, Hemingway, Henry Green, Elizabeth Bowen, Anthony Powell.

"How did they hold up?" I asked cheerfully.

"Not at all," he told me. "They feel like completely empty performances. Like it wasn't worth it at all."

Coming out, it felt like I'd just been to a very challenging tutorial.

CHANGING OUR STORIES

CAN PEOPLE CHANGE their lives? Can novelists change the kind of stories they write?

The two questions are not unrelated. I raise them after reading a long (thoughtful, generous) review of my own novel writing, which, nevertheless, seems perplexed by a shift in the content and credo of my recent work. Until a couple of years ago, the reviewer observes, Parks's novels were remorseless in suggesting that we are who we are who we are, can't change, character is destiny, family is destiny, habits of mind are destiny; the kind of job we do, the person we share our lives with, the ongoing stories we are involved in are all so much part of ourselves that any thought of changing them inevitably drags us toward madness and self-destruction.

The reviewer evidently admires the rigor of this position, and feels a little let down when in my nonfiction work *Teach Us to Sit Still*, then again in my recent novel *Sex is Forbidden*, there is some movement away from it. As if it might be a weakness to step back a little and wonder: Is all this determinism really true? Is this unhappy thing really necessary, and not just another burdensome piece of lumber I have become attached to? Do I really have to stay in this job, this marriage, this town, forever?

Above all, the reviewer doesn't consider the possibility that, in the presence of an urgent desire for change, as there clearly was for the characters he talks about in the earlier novels, the conviction that one can't change might be, on the character's part, and perhaps on the author's too, a way of blocking oneself, preventing oneself from moving on, of finding excuses for inaction, or of ennobling pain ("I would like to change, but alas life is not like that"). It's certainly a formula that allows for much drama and pathos.

This doesn't mean, of course, that writers and the characters they create don't genuinely hold this belief, or at least take it seriously. On the contrary, they have to take it seriously, otherwise they really would move toward change. Nor does it mean that there aren't perhaps special reasons why readers would keep coming back to an author who believes change impossible; perhaps they themselves, like the author, have an investment in this position. Imagine discovering some unpublished work by Fitzgerald in which a Gatsby figure very easily recovers his lost love from her crass billionaire husband and sets up a happy home with her across the water from her ex. There was no real problem after all. Or a Faulkner novel where the suffocating paralysis of the Southern past just falls away following a smart if painful decision to move West, stop drinking, and accept the pleasures that a charming new lover is offering, someone entirely unimpressed by the torments of Yoknapatawpha County.

I want to put forward this provocation, not for the sake of stirring the water, but because I have begun to suspect it is true: most of our finest narratives, films as well as novels, however formally innovative and politically anti-establishment, are actually conservative, even inhibiting, in their consequences and implications. Shortly before writing *The Return of the Native*, Hardy copies down a paragraph from Heinrich Heine:

Modern times find themselves with an immense system of institutions, established facts, accredited dogmas, customs, rules,
which have come to them from times not modern. In this system their life has to be carried forward; yet they have a sense
that this system is not of their own creation, that it by no means
corresponds exactly with the wants of their actual life, that, for
them, it is customary, not rational. The awakening of this sense
is the awakening of the modern spirit.

But he also jots down this warning remark from Theodore Watts:

Science tells us that, in the struggle for life, the surviving organ-
ism is not necessarily that which is absolutely the best in an
ideal sense, though it must be that which is most in harmony
with surrounding conditions.

He then goes on to write the first of a series of novels where all the
"best" people are destroyed as their impulse toward self-realization
collides with constricting conventions, economic hardship, and prej-
udice of every kind. This while Hardy himself struggled to remain in
a marriage that was increasingly arid and continued to attend church
regularly despite being an atheist.

Writers producing novels that follow this formula—and they are
legion—are often praised for identifying and attacking the forces responsible for destroying their characters' lives and denying them self-
realization. They are considered progressive. Yet the question remains
whether this message of the inevitability of defeat—"the time was not
ripe for us," says Hardy's *Jude*, "our ideas were fifty years too soon"
—is actually a form of consolation, a bid to improve self-esteem, or,
more corrosively, an invitation not to try. It would surely make sense,

after all, in a world that gives the maximum importance to individual emancipation but at the same time is so complex and interconnected as to be dependent on a certain uniformity of behavior, that we would develop narratives that flatter our individual "progressive" spirit but discourage us from acting on it.

What I'm trying to suggest here is, first: There are always reasons why an author (or simply a person) tells and keeps telling a certain kind of story, in a certain style, with a certain outcome. And I don't just mean reasons that lie behind the story's genesis, but also reasons that have to do with future consequences of seeing life this way; the story, and the conviction it carries, are part of the teller's way of organizing his own life. Second: Readers are not neutral observers of this, not, I mean, engaged in savoring fine prose and well-structured narrative in a purely aesthetic way. However distant the actual plot may be from your experience, the story nevertheless intersects with your life: it can be reassuring, unnerving, boring, exciting, challenging, unbelievable; it can make you impatient; it can be helpful or unhelpful.

It's precisely for this reason, precisely because of the power of narrative to shift or at least threaten our attitudes, to stymie us, that there are times when you might want to avoid certain books as unhelpful. Just as you don't consult a pessimist when planning a major career move, so it would hardly be wise to give Chekhov's short stories to the partner you have just proposed to. And you certainly don't want to be reading *Tess of the D'Urbervilles* or *Jude the Obscure* while planning a family. Literature is not neutral.

Still, some writers do change their stories and their style quite decisively: Dickens shifted abruptly from optimism to pessimism, T. S. Eliot from a grumbling gloom to something approaching serenity, Joyce from relative simplicity to unspeakable complexity, Beckett from baroque English to the sparest French, Hardy from novels to poetry, or indeed, in the case of one of my favorite writers, Henry Green, from regular writing to silence. In each case, if one examines the life of the author, it becomes clear that the earlier approach no longer "worked" for the writer, no longer contained the tensions that need to be contained in order to go on living in a certain way. Some other story was necessary. Or alternatively, change had happened, had been achieved, for better or worse, and the previous story was simply no longer appropriate, because no longer required.

I recall in this regard a recent conversation with a young novelist who was in some distress about his private life, in particular his obviously conflicted behavior with women. I encouraged him to see an analyst and hopefully sort things out. He said he had thought about this but was concerned that a successful analysis would alter the way he wrote, his ability to write tense, distraught stories about conflicted behavior with women, etc. I laughed. When despair brings home the bacon and self-esteem with it, it's hard to let it go. "When you are suffering enough," I suggested, "I mean so much that it's simply impossible to go on, then something will give and the stories will change, like it or not."

So, to return to the reviewer of my novels: when a writer like myself, who has preached the inevitability of destiny and the impossibility of change for so long, begins to write rather different stories and look for new versions of events, you can feel free to assume that the old "narrative strategy" hasn't delivered the desired results, or no longer delivers them. He's no longer able to hold things together as they were by telling himself and the world there's no other solution. The reader too, the faithful generous reader, who came back again and again to those unhappy tales and found sustenance in them, might take timely warning.

WRITING TO DEATH

HOW FAR IS the trajectory of an author's writing career and the themes that guide it related to the moment and nature of his or her death?

I have suggested that much great narrative writing springs from some unresolved conflict, or we might even say, structural dilemma in the author's personality. Thomas Hardy yearns for the courage to be free but has been brought up as a feeble mother's boy, constantly reminded of his frailty. All his life he will go back and forth between the adventure and freedom of London and the safety and constriction of his native Dorset; to London when confident, back to mother when in crisis (returns often preceded by a mystery illness). Frustrated in his marriage, Hardy writes of people who yearn to break society's rules, above all be with the partner they desire, but are invariably destroyed when they actually try to do so, as if these novels were a message to himself not to risk it. Yet Hardy always stopped short of pushing personal problems to crisis, and when his wife died was well placed to marry his live-in secretary, almost forty years younger than himself. Never solving his dilemmas, but always finding some solution that avoided self-destruction, he lived to a ripe old eighty-seven.

In his long study of Hardy's work, D. H. Lawrence spurned the older writer's caution and found his novels as poisonous in their implications as they were admirable in their writing. Caught at an early age in a similar impasse between fear and courage, Lawrence resolved that every form of limitation, whether imposed by self or society, is a sin against nature. One *must* seize what one justly wants. No matter what. Courage is a duty, conformity a vice. Running off with a married woman, mother of three children, Lawrence invariably sought out conflict, embracing the things he still nevertheless feared. Often he delighted in imagining the outraged reviews that would inevitably result from whatever he was writing. Suffering from lung problems from an early age, he was as uncompromising with his health as he was with censorship, conformism, or inhibition. He would not accept that he had TB, and took no medical advice until it was far too late. Apparently, the solution to his early personal dilemma, which demanded freedom at all costs, did not allow him to discriminate between different kinds of constrictions. Working nonstop, traveling recklessly, he died at forty-four. A late poem has him fitting out a ship to sail toward death.

Chekhov is another who denied that he had TB and seemed to do everything to make it worse, an attitude that was all the more curious because he was himself a doctor. His work invariably shows characters torn between the need to belong to a family or social group and the fear of being imprisoned in it, of losing life's intensity in trivial routine. Putting himself at the center of his family of origin, buying or building generous houses for his parents and siblings, he would then have a small annex built for himself near the larger home so as to remain separate from them. Flirting constantly with marriageable girls, he carefully avoided marriage and when hard pressed by the beautiful Lika Mizinova embarked on an extremely arduous journey to Sakhalin, an island penitentiary off the coast of Siberia, where he contemplated those trapped and brutalized in Russia's worst prison community. The writing itself became a way both of being at the heart of Russian society, but also apart from it, taking no sides on political issues, writing things people didn't expect, above all writing short stories, preferably very short, thus avoiding the imprisoning commitment of the great Russian novel.

As it progressed, Chekhov's illness sharpened his dilemma: to seek treatment or ask for help would mean submitting to routine and restriction, which he restlessly avoided. To live intensely, as he wanted, would speed up the illness and shorten the life available. In 1901 at forty-one, now ill beyond any denial and forced to live in the warm climate of the Black Sea, Chekhov married a lively and successful actress who worked in Moscow. The frequent trips from the hot dull (as he saw it) south to the freezing and frenetic capital were, his doctor observed, the worst thing he could do for his sickness. And indeed so many of Chekhov's characters seem to make the worst possible, if not suicidal, choices. Having spoken, in April 1904, of going to the front line of the Russian-Japanese war to get a view of the action, Chekhov died in a hotel room in the German spa town of Badenweiler where he had finally agreed to seek treatment.

It is not that I believe that one pattern fits all, simply that so many of the writers I have looked at seem permanently torn between irreconcilable positions, something that seems to feed that famous ambiguity literary critics so much admire; eventually, the dilemma driving the work either leads to death, or is neutralized in a way that prolongs life but dulls the writing. Dickens, father figure par excellence and great promoter of the happy family, writes novels that draw people of every class into a sense of national belonging, yet he simultaneously feels drastically let down by wife, children, publishers, friends, sometimes even readers. Firing his wife, mother of his ten children, he takes up with a young mistress who must be kept hidden, since what kind of identity can Dickens have if he is not Britain's favorite and very respectable family author?

The grim later novels—*Little Dorrit, Our Mutual Friend*—express in all kinds of ways the impossibility of balancing these conflicting impulses. They are books of greater scope and seriousness than the earlier work, yet at the same time dissatisfying or disturbing in their failure to resolve these conflicts even aesthetically. In his fifties, shortly after pushing his wife out of the home and against the advice of his doctors, Dickens launched into one reading tour after another, often performing for hours night after night, becoming the center of attention for rapturous audiences. This was meat and drink to him, but raised even higher the cost of any revelation of his private circumstances. After the readings came the grueling journeys to arrive at wherever he had hidden his mistress, between Paris and London. Drinking heavily the while, Dickens did not surprise doctors, friends, or family when he collapsed and died at fifty-eight.

Before one last example, let me be more precise. What I am suggesting is that a novelist's work is often a strategy (I don't mean the author need be aware of this) for dealing with some personal dilemma. Not just that the dilemma is "worked out" in the narrative, as critics often tell us, but that the acts of writing and publishing and positioning oneself in the world of literature are all part of an attempt to find a solution, however provisional, to some deep personal unease. In many cases, however hard the writing is pushed, the solution is indeed only temporary or partial, and both author and work eventually succumb. Obviously the easiest group of authors to look at in this regard would be the suicides, Virginia Woolf, Cesare Pavese, David Foster Wallace. But to finish, let's consider William Faulkner.

Throughout his life, when asked for biographical details Faulkner would begin by saying he was the great grandson of the Old Colonel, a man renowned for his courage, temper, energy, and vision—and a writer to boot. In contrast Faulkner saw his own father as a nobody and a loser, an opinion he seemed to share with his mother, to whom he remained close throughout his life, having coffee with her most afternoons and never missing a family Christmas if he could help it. From his earliest days he was eager to present himself as bold and courageous, inventing in 1918 a bizarre story of having crashed a warplane while celebrating the end of the war. For years he affected a limp supposedly resulting from the crash, though at the time he had never piloted a plane at all. His brother was actually wounded in the war. Faulkner's first novel focuses on a soldier returning home a hero, but so badly wounded that he dies.

Like Thomas Hardy, Faulkner eventually invented a fictional territory of his own where his novels could all take place in relation to each other. Acts of courage in Yoknapatawpha County—usually a very physical, manly courage, but also the courage to claim the woman you really desire—end up, as in Hardy's novels, in wounds, disaster, and death. Like Hardy, Faulkner married a woman he was eager to betray (and did) but never able to walk out on. Community in the South is presented as a tremendous, insuperable burden that one can neither escape nor overcome. The only freedom available is the freedom, the courage, to live slightly apart, not to engage with the world or women, like Ike McCaslin, hero of *The Bear*.

Over the years Faulkner's writing became both a solution to and a representation of the conflicting impulses that tormented him. His stylistic experimentalism became an act of courage in itself, allowing him to criticize the genuinely war-wounded and mythically courageous Hemingway for not being brave enough to experiment with his writing and risk failure. Yet Faulkner's experimentation is never liberating: his prose gives us the impression of a wild, would-be heroic energy pushing through an impossibly dense medium, shoving aside negative after negative to reach the brief respite of a positive verb, losing itself in a heavy slime of ancestors and ancient wrongs. It is not a world in which one could hope to become the courageous man

Faulkner wished to be. From the black community, Faulkner told a friend, we can learn "resignation."

One major difference between the patterns that guide Hardy's and Faulkner's work is the latter's relationship with alcohol, which, more than a mere disinhibitor making courage possible, becomes a sort of courage in itself. However adventurous and ferociously provocative, Faulkner's writing was not enough to satisfy his need to feel courageous. Throughout his life he drank epically, heroically. In the hunting camp that is the setting of *The Bear* we hear that

> the bottle was always present, so that after a while it seemed to him that those fierce instants of heart and brain and courage and wiliness and speed were concentrated and distilled into that brown liquor which not women, not boys and children, but only hunters drank, drinking not of the blood they had spilled but some condensation of the wild immortal spirit, drinking it moderately, humbly even, not with the pagan's base hope of acquiring the virtues of cunning and strength and speed, but in salute to them.

Whiskey and writing intertwine throughout Faulkner's life, feeding each other, blocking each other, never allowing him to achieve any stability, always acting out a salute to other men he feared he could not resemble. By the time he was fifty the end seemed inevitable. There are only so many times one can dry out in a clinic and fall drunk off a horse. It was actually something of a miracle that Faulkner outlived his dear mother for a year before one more courageous binge, one more salute to the truly brave, as he saw it, did him in, aged sixty-four.

IV
Writing Across Worlds

"ARE YOU THE TIM PARKS WHO...?"

WHAT THE POETS of the ancient world feared most was exile, alienation from their community. This was the punishment of Seneca, Ovid, Catullus, and many others. It wasn't that they were incapable of learning another language and addressing a different audience; just that it made little sense to do so. Their work had meaning in relation to the community to which they belonged.

To what community does a writer belong today? The whole world, might seem to be the obvious answer in an era of globalization. Alas, it's not that simple. Take my own case. I am known in England mainly for light, though hopefully thoughtful nonfiction; in Italy for polemical newspaper articles and a controversial book about soccer; in Germany, Holland, and France for what I consider my "serious" novels *Europa*, *Destiny*, *Cleaver*; in the United States for literary criticism; and in a smattering of other countries, but also in various academic communities, for my translations and writing on translation. Occasionally I receive emails that ask, "But are you also the Tim Parks who...?" Frequently readers get my nationality wrong. They don't seem to know where I'm coming from or headed to.

How can something like this happen in a world where information is supposed to flow so freely? The key, I suppose, is never to enjoy huge success in any of the fields you work in. Chance, modern communications, and an urgent need to earn money can do the rest. In 1979 I married an Italian; in 1981, aged twenty-six and already writing novels that were regularly rejected, I moved to Italy. Unable to publish, I translated, first commercially, then, with a lucky break, novels. At last in 1985 a novel of my own was published in London and I began to build up a small reputation as a novelist. However, my living in Italy prompted publishers to ask me to write about the place, luring me with offers of "a great deal more money than you will ever earn with the kind of novels you write." After ten years I gave in, writing first about the street I lived in and some years later about Italian children, schools, and families. It was great fun and all at once I was Mr. Italy.

But if this reputation made sense to the English—one of their ilk decoding another country—it didn't attract the Germans, Dutch, and French who seemed to feel that serious novel writing was not compatible with this kind of ironic anthropology. In Germany, where my novels were outselling English editions by many times, the critics invited me to intensely earnest debates on Europe and fiction, and in general everybody felt it would be unwise to insist too much on this other material. I was now quite different people in England, Germany, and Italy, where I had begun to write newspaper articles in Italian on Italian issues for Italians, without the framing and contextualizing needed when talking about such matters to those who don't know the country. Then, while all this was going on and for reasons I have never fathomed, *The New York Review of Books* invited me to write about Italian authors and books on Italy; a long collaboration began, I convinced the *Review* that I could also write about matters non-Italian, and my image in the USA, if one can speak so grandly, became radically different than it was elsewhere. I was an essayist.

Why do I feel this state of affairs is interesting? We think of globalization as drawing more and more people into a single community where readers all over the world read the same authors. The process is hardly new, more like an acceleration with greatly empowered means of an old propensity toward connection, communication, acquisition, appropriation, aggregation. Since earliest times communities expanded, swallowed each other up, or were swallowed, became more aware of and curious about those neighboring communities too big to beat. The writer whose community was destroyed was finished. Who would listen, even if he could speak their tongue? He was irrelevant. Others more fortunate found themselves with a larger and larger community to address: the court, the burghers, a growing group of cultured men, eventually the middle classes, and finally the people. Now there was also the possibility that somebody in another country, seeing your local fame, might grow interested, might translate your work.

Huge numbers of languages, great riches and diversity were lost in this process, which allowed larger societies to form so that eventually a single writer was in a position to speak to thousands, millions, even tens of millions. At this point writers were competing to be one of the chosen few who would enjoy the privilege of selling their work to much larger, though necessarily looser and more fragmented communities. Some began to see this as a form of freedom; not to be fatally attached to one homogeneous group, not to risk extinction as a writer if your community, your peers, rejected you. The day came when writers actually sought out exile, left voluntarily, and were proud of it. Byron, Shelley, Lawrence, Joyce—they stood outside the societies that had made them and became in their own lifetimes international figures. Yet they continued to write toward and mostly against the nations that bred them, and their international success depended on their notoriety in their home countries.

We still feel this is the normal model for literature. At the Nobel level it is very unusual to give the prize to a writer who has not already won laurels in his own country. For popular fiction, Stephen King, Dan Brown, J. K. Rowling, and Stieg Larsson all follow a similar pattern: a book is phenomenally successful at home, other countries buy into it (which can happen very rapidly now), as the sales mount up, a promotions machine gears up to support them, projecting the same image of the author worldwide as was projected at home. The effect is to sever the umbilical chord, if not the relationship, with the home community. Writers like Dan Brown and J. K. Rowling cannot be exiled. They have readers everywhere.

But globalization is not uniform and not always so kind. It can happen that a writer remains absolutely trapped in his local community, perhaps well known for a restricted group, but unable to project him or herself outside it. I think of the fine South Tyrolese novelist Joseph Zoderer, who yearns to be an international novelist and has had his work translated in some countries, but never in English, and who finds himself constantly labeled as a Tyrolese writer. To publish successfully he has to write toward this community; when he seeks to write about matters outside it, neither his own community nor the outer world are interested. Likewise there are many writers from ex-colonies or simply the developing world who find they have to address the Western world about their now distant home; publishers are immediately less interested if they seek to address other issues (I have heard this from a successful young Chinese novelist in London, and from a Surinamese in Holland). I say "have to" with the implied condition, if they want to be well and traditionally published. It is our desire for money and celebrity that binds us.

But my own case is, I think, more curious, and I would be eager to hear of other writers in the same position, or rather many positions. Inevitably, as one addresses different communities of readers in different countries one tends to write differently for them, not necessarily to please, but just to be in meaningful relation to them. In fact if I want to displease them, I have to be very aware of their likes and dislikes. I don't do this with cynical calculation. It simply happens, like an adjustment to the weather, or the language you are speaking, or your new girlfriend's parents; and you discover you are a different writer, a different person almost, when engaging in different projects. This can be quite liberating and certainly more fun than the writer who feels trapped in a small world. You realize you are many writers, potentially very many, and the way your talents develop will depend on the way different communities in different countries respond to you.

This reality is in sharp contrast with the rhetoric that surrounds creative writing today. If asked, most writers will say they write only for themselves and are not aware of, let alone swayed by an audience. An ideal notion of globalization, then, posits this sovereign individual, who enjoys a consistent and absolute identity, above any contamination from those who buy his work, selling the product of his or her genius to a world that is able to receive it and enjoy it in the same way everywhere. So individualism and globalization go hand in glove. The idea that we are absolutely free of any community permits us to engage with all people everywhere. This is why so much international literature is about freedom and favors rebellions against institutions.

But the experience of the writer addressing multiple separate audiences—or perhaps using pseudonyms for certain kinds of writing in contrast with the work published under his or her own name—belies this myth. Indeed, as the years go by, I begin to suspect that it is precisely in positing themselves as independent from and uninfluenced by the collective, that writers are in fact agreeing to fill a part that the modern community of would-be individuals has dreamt up for them: the one who allows us all to believe that freedom and absolute identity outside the community are possible.

UGLY AMERICANS ABROAD

I'M ENGLISH AND live in Italy. During March 2011, within two or three days of each other, I received: from *The New York Review of Books*, four novels by the Swiss author Peter Stamm; from the Italian newspaper *Il Sole 24 Ore*, Jonathan Franzen's *Freedom*, in English and Italian; and from a New York publisher, a first novel, *Funeral for a Dog*, by the young German writer Thomas Pletzinger. The last was accompanied by some promotional puff that began: "Pletzinger is German, but you wouldn't know it from his debut, which is both wise and worldly."

What a wonderful insight this careless moment of blurb-talk gives us into the contemporary American mindset! We want something worldly, but if it seems too German, or perhaps just too foreign, we become wary. As my mailbag indicates, the literary community is very much an international phenomenon, but not, it would seem, a level playing field. To make it in America, Pletzinger must shed his German-ness as if he were an immigrant with an embarrassing accent.

Peter Stamm, whose novels I eventually reviewed, rises to this challenge with great ingenuity. He writes in the leanest prose imaginable, telling stories about phobic characters in love with routine, in need of protection, but simultaneously anxious that life might be passing them by; they yearn for life and are afraid of it, and the more they yearn, the more they are afraid. Stamm's genius is to align his spare prose with the psychology of people who fear richness and density; that way he creates a style that's both "literary" and absolutely translatable:

> Andreas loved the empty mornings when he would stand by the window with a cup of coffee in one hand and a cigarette in the other, and stare down at the small, tidy courtyard, and think about nothing except what was there in front of him: a small rectangular bed in the middle of the courtyard, planted with ivy with a tree in it, that put out a few thin branches, pruned to fit the small space that was available.

If you didn't know Stamm was Swiss, nothing in the English translation would betray this blemish. Certainly he never tells you anything about Switzerland, or the other countries where his books are set. Whenever one of his main characters is asked, while abroad, about his or her home country, the wry Stamm has them shrug and answer that they don't really have anything to say.

Franzen is the opposite; he could hardly be more loudly American, and to come to him right after Stamm is to see how different are the roads to celebrity for the Swiss author and the American. While Stamm's characters come free, or bereft, of any social or political context, Franzen's often seem barely distinguishable from a dense background cluttered with product names, detailed history and geography, linguistic tics, dress habits, and so on, all described with a mixture of irony and disdain, an assumption of superiority and distance, that I immediately find myself uncomfortable with.

Lists abound in *Freedom*: to describe the meanness of the grandparents of Patty, the protagonist, we are given a list of the "insulting gifts" they bring at Christmas:

> Joyce famously one year received two much used dish towels. Ray typically got one of those big art books from the Barnes & Noble bargain table, sometimes with a $3.99 sticker still on it. The kids got little pieces of plastic Asian-made crap: tiny travel alarm clocks that didn't work, coin purses stamped with the name of a New Jersey insurance agency, frightening crude Chinese finger puppets, assorted swizzle sticks.

Every character trait, every room, every neighborhood, is good for a list, as if Franzen himself were eager to overwhelm us with gifts of dubious taste:

> By summer's end, Blake had nearly finished work on the greatroom and was outfitting it with such Blakean gear as PlayStation, Foosball, a refrigerated beer keg, a large-screen TV, an air-hockey table, a stained-glass Vikings chandelier, and mechanized recliners.

Often it feels like the characters only exist as an alibi for what is really a journalistic and encyclopedic endeavor to list everything American. Where it's not objects, it's behavior patterns:

> In the days after 9/11, everything suddenly seemed extremely stupid to Joey. It was stupid that a "Vigil of Concern" was held for no conceivable practical reason, it was stupid that people kept watching the same disaster footage over and over, it was stupid that the Chi Phi boys hung a banner of "support" from their house, it was stupid that the football game against Penn

State was canceled, it was stupid that so many kids left Grounds to be with their families (and it was stupid that everybody at Virginia said "Grounds" instead of "campus").

It's interesting that in this passage the Italian translator has to leave words like *football* (as opposed to soccer), then *Grounds*, and *campus*, in English. This alerts us to a larger problem with translating Franzen; these are not just lists of American things and things American people do, but also—and crucially—of the very words Americans use. Foosball, or table football in British English, is called *calcio balilla* in Italian, Balilla being the nickname of a child hero who in 1746 started a revolution by throwing stones at Austrian soldiers. The translator rightly shies away from using a term that would shift the mind abruptly toward Italian culture, leaving the incomprehensible Foosball. Further on, Italian has neither the object nor the denomination "mechanized recliners," so the translator is obliged to explain what it is (and the reader still won't be able to picture this aberration in all its ugliness).

For the American reader, there is the pleasure of recognizing the interiors Franzen so meticulously describes, while the English reader can just about hang on with all he has learned from films and TV. Not so for the Italian, or German, or Frenchman, who simply struggles through lists of alien bric-a-brac. We might say that if the Swiss Stamm, to attract an international public, has been obliged to write about everyman for everyone everywhere, Franzen, thanks to the size of America's internal market, but also to the huge pull the country exercises on the world's imagination, can write about Americans for Americans (which is no doubt as it should be) and nevertheless expect to be read worldwide.

Aside from the recognition factor—this is America—are there other pleasures to be had from Franzen, pleasures available to the foreigner reading in translation? I knew before opening it, of course, that *Freedom* was "an important novel" if only because *The Guardian* had dedicated to it an article on its homepage (on which my browser opens). Even before he had read the book, the *Guardian* writer remarked that Franzen was probably the only novelist alive able to revive our belief in the literary novel. Traveling in Holland the week the English edition was published, I saw that Amsterdam's main international bookshop had dedicated their entire window to it.

At a loss to understand this enthusiasm (I found the novel hard going), I checked out *The New York Times Book Review* where Sam Tanenhaus canonizes the novel in his first sentence; it is "a masterpiece of American fiction." Interesting here is the word *American*. To be a masterpiece of American fiction is to have hit the top. "A masterpiece of Swiss fiction" does not have the same ring, and if, say, a work by Pamuk is declared a masterpiece it will not be "a masterpiece of Turkish fiction." Tanenhaus then quickly explains Franzen's achievement, which is to gather up "every fresh datum of our shared millennial life." He goes on:

> Franzen knows that college freshmen are today called "first years," like tender shoots in an overplanted garden; that a high-minded mom, however ruthless in her judgments of her neighbors' ethical lapses, will condemn them with no epithet harsher than "weird"; that reckless drivers who barrel across lanes are "almost always youngish men for whom the use of blinkers was apparently an affront to their masculinity."

Is it really such an achievement to know that "freshmen" are called "first years" (as in most places in the world for that matter)? The plot is described as "intricately ordered" and Franzen's one prominent formal device (having the main character Patty relate much of the

book as a third-person autobiography on the prompting of her thera-
pist) as "ingenious." Neither is true. The plot is a complete pig's
ear—to use a very English if not American expression—and is best
grasped by checking out John Crace's hilarious "Digested read,"
again in *The Guardian*. As for the voice, the supposedly unsophisti-
cated jock, Patty, turns out to have a style that is undistinguishable
from that of the extremely sophisticated Franzen; it is never clear
what the story gains from pretending that she is telling it. On the
contrary, the move undermines the novel's credibility.

But *Freedom*'s failings are interesting in so far as they deepen the
mystery of the book's international success. It's one thing for the
Americans to hype and canonize one of their favorite authors, but
why do the Europeans buy into it? Ever anxious that they need to
understand America, fascinated by its glamour and power, Europeans
are perhaps attracted to those American novels that explain everything: Roth's *American Pastoral*, DeLillo's *Underworld*. More than
a novel by an American, they want The Great American Novel. But
of course Europeans also resent American world hegemony and feel
(still and no doubt wrongly) superior culturally.

Freedom has this characteristic: Franzen appears to get all his energy, all his identity, from simultaneously evoking and disdaining
America, explaining it (its gaucheness mostly) and rejecting it; his
stories invariably offer characters engaging in the American world,
finding themselves tainted and debased by it, then at last coming to
their Franzenesque "corrected" senses and withdrawing from it.
Blinded by this or that ambition, they come to grief because they lack
knowledge, they lack awareness. Thus the importance of so much
information. Unlike his characters, Franzen knows everything, is
aware of everything, and aware above all that redemption lies in
withdrawal from the American public scene. What message could be
more welcome to Europeans? A friend writes to me from Berlin and

remarks, "Here in Germany, Franzen's the only American novelist people talk about." That is, Franzen is establishing a picture of a dysfunctional America that Europeans feel happy with. With Franzen they can "do" America and have done with it.

YOUR ENGLISH IS SHOWING

IS ENGLISH, AND specifically American English, destined to take over the world?

The recent acceleration in communications and the process we've grown used to calling globalization have renewed an old debate about the relationship between lingua franca and vernacular. The nations of the European mainland are constantly anxious that the adoption of English words and even syntactical structures may be seriously reshaping their languages. Meanwhile, in many technical fields, scientific papers are now written almost exclusively in English, with the result that certain concepts become difficult to express in the local vernacular since no one is at work developing a vocabulary for them.

Back in 2000, in an intriguing article titled "Cosmopolitan and Vernacular in History," Sheldon Pollock discussed the possible ways a lingua franca can relate to different vernaculars by comparing the fortunes of Latin and other languages in the Roman Empire with those of Sanskrit and local languages in India and the East during the same period (roughly from the beginning of the first millennium to its end). His general claim is that while in the West Latin was ruthlessly imposed on the back of Roman military conquest and tended to obliterate the languages of peoples subdued, in the East there was a more relaxed coexistence between the cosmopolitan lingua franca and the surrounding vernaculars, Sanskrit gaining a general currency more through trade and a desire to be widely understood than through military conquest or political coercion.

The burden of Pollock's article is clear enough: that we needn't think about the spread of English as necessarily in conflict with the world's vernaculars; he wants us to avoid thinking in terms of "either/or" and work toward a relationship that is "both/and." The advice is good, and more than a dozen years later the article is as intriguing as ever, though perhaps what struck me most on a recent rereading was the contemporaneous nature of these linguistic experiences in East and West: both saw the rise and decline of a lingua franca at more or less the same time, suggesting the working out of an underlying process and the manifestation of a collective will.

But reading about translation and international literature, reading novels in translation from many nations, and also reading the work of graduate students of translation and creative writing, I have gathered the impression that we are heading for a new and rather different resolution of the tension between lingua franca and vernacular. While easily conceding that certain areas of highly specialized knowledge become the exclusive domain of English, most people are not so willing, nor able, to read novels, or indeed any prose that involves strong elements of style, in a foreign language. There they want to keep to their mother tongue. Nor are many creative writers able and willing to follow in the footsteps of a Conrad or Nabokov, or more recently the many Asian and Indian writers who have switched from their native tongues to more marketable English. Most writers want to go on writing in their own languages.

Yet at the same time, neither readers nor writers are happy any longer with the idea that a literary text's nation or language of origin should in any way define or limit the area in which it moves, or indeed that a national audience be the first and perhaps only arbiter of a book's destiny. We feel far too linked up these days not to want to know which books are being read in which other countries right now. And if we are writers, of course, we want our own books to travel as widely as possible.

The obvious solution is translation. And indeed, there has never been so much translation as there is today, nor has it ever happened so soon after publication of the original, with groups of translators sweating over typescripts of blockbuster thrillers or even literary novels so that they can be published at the same time in many countries with a simultaneous and unified promotional campaign. Few people realize how many books are now translated by more than one translator (often this is not made clear in the credits), nor how fast translators are expected to work. It might be argued that the literary world is merely following the cinema with its international distribution circuits. But books are not films. While most films can survive subtitling or dubbing, the success of translation very largely depends on the levels of complexity in the original text. Above all there is a problem with a kind of writing that is, as it were, inward-turning, about the language itself, about what it means to live under the spell of this or that vernacular.

Of course one can translate Joyce's *Ulysses*, but one loses the book's reveling in its own linguistic medium, its tireless exploration of the possibilities of English. The same is true of a lot of the experimental writing of the 1960s and 1970s. It is desperately hard to translate the Flemish writer Hugo Claus into English, or indeed Thomas Pynchon's *Gravity's Rainbow* into anything. There was a mining of linguistic richness in that period, and a focus on the extent to which our culture is made up of words, that tended to exclude, or simply wasn't concerned about, the question of having a text that can travel the world. Even practitioners of "traditional" realism such as John Updike or, in England and in a quite different way, Barbara Pym, were obsessively attentive to the exact form of words that was their culture. In many ways Pym is untranslatable into Italian, or rather translation so alters the tone of the work that it's hard to think of it as by Pym at all.

It was when I was invited to review in the same article a new translation of Hugo Claus's *Wonder* (1962) alongside Per Petterson's *Out Stealing Horses* (2003) and Gerbrand Bakker's *The Twin* (2006) that it occurred to me that over the forty years between Claus and the others an important change had occurred. These more recent novels had, yes, been translated, from Norwegian and Dutch into English, but it was nothing like the far more arduous task of translating Claus and many of his peers. Rather, it seemed that the contemporary writers had already performed a translation within their own languages; they had discovered a lingua franca within their own vernacular, a particular straightforwardness, an agreed order for saying things and perceiving and reporting experience, that made translation easier and more effective. One might call it a simplification, or one might call it an alignment in different languages to an agreed way of going about things.

Inevitably, there is an impoverishment. Neither of these authors have the mad fertility of Claus; but there is also a huge gain in communicability, particularly in translation where the rhythm of delivery and the immediacy of expression are free from any sense of obstacle. Is it possible, I asked myself, that there is now a skeleton lingua franca beneath the flesh of these vernaculars, and that it is basically an English skeleton?

Of course as soon as one has excited oneself with an idea, one finds confirmation of it everywhere. As I have observed, Peter Stamm very much fits this description, likewise the German Siegfried Lenz, and many other French and Italian authors. So strong is the flavor of English in the Italian of the bestselling thriller writer Giorgio Faletti that a number of readers suggested it was actually translated from an English original written by someone else. At my own university in Milan, we have a project called GLINT (Global Literature and Translation) of which one area involves studying the extent to which Italian syntax has shifted toward English models over the last fifty years. There is no shortage of evidence. Contemporary Italian more frequently puts the adjective before the noun, more frequently uses possessives for parts of the body, more frequently introduces a pro-noun subject, and more frequently uses the present progressive, all changes that suggest an influence from English.

So that is the intuition. The idea is not so much the old polemic that English is simply dominant and dangerous; but rather that there is a spirit abroad, especially in the world of fiction, that is seeking maximum communicability and that has fastened onto the world's present lingua franca as something that can be absorbed and built into other vernaculars so that they can continue to exist while be-coming more easily translated into each other—or into English itself.

One may see this as a wise compromise between lingua franca and vernacular, or as a slow caving-in to rampant English. Certainly it's hard not to regret the dazzling and very Italian density of an author like Carlo Emilio Gadda, whose work is still only inadequately trans-lated. On the other hand it's intriguing to see that in resistance to the general drift toward the international—a game of polarities if you like, where one trend is confirmed by the extent to which it provokes its opposite—there is also a flourishing of dialect poetry, texts com-prehensible only by a very small community. (I cannot understand the poetry of my close colleague Edoardo Zuccato, who writes in the

Milanese dialect.) But such poetry is almost always published with an Italian translation alongside it, suggesting the poet's desire for intimacy and authenticity on the one hand and an eagerness, perhaps anxiety, to be widely understood on the other. Any eventual translations, of course, will be made from the Italian, not the dialect.

LEARNING TO SPEAK AMERICAN

IN 1993 I translated all 450 pages of Roberto Calasso's *The Marriage of Cadmus and Harmony* without ever using the past participle of the verb *get*. The book was to be published simultaneously by Knopf in New York and Jonathan Cape in London; to save money, both editions were to be printed from the same galleys, so it would be important, I was told, to avoid any usages that might strike American readers as distractingly English or English readers as distractingly American. To my English ear *gotten* yells America and alters the whole feel of a sentence. I presumed it would be the same the other way round for Americans. Fortunately, given the high register of Calasso's prose, *get* was not difficult to avoid.

Now, two decades later, I am obliged to sign up to *gotten*. Commissioned by an American publisher to write a book that explores the Italian national character through an account of thirty years' commuting and traveling on the country's rail network, I am looking at an edit that transforms my English prose into American. I had already sorted out the spelling, in fact had written the book with an American spell check, and didn't expect that there would be much else to do. Wrong. Almost at once there was a note saying that throughout the three hundred pages my use of *carriage* for a passenger train car must be changed to *coach*. Since this is a book about trains and train travel there were ninety-eight such usages. There was also the problem that I had used the word *coach* to refer to a long-distance bus. Apparently the twenty-four-hour clock was not acceptable, so the 17:25 Regionale from Milan to Verona had to become the 5:25 PM Regionale. Where I, in a discussion of prices, had written "a further 50 cents" the American edit required "a further 50 euro cents," as if otherwise an American reader might imagine Italians were dealing in nickels and dimes.

I had started the editing process in a spirit of easygoing cooperation, determined to set aside any pride in Englishness and work to produce the best package possible for an American public. After all, the work was being paid for by an American publisher, and my commissioning editor had proved extremely helpful when it came to discussing the shape of the book. But doubts soon arose. Prose is not something that remains the same when words are substituted—*jeans* for *dungarees*, for example—or when one synonym is preferred to another. Rhythm is important, and assonance likewise. Ninety-eight uses of a two-syllable *carriage* are not the same as ninety-eight occurrences of a single-syllable closed-*o coach*. This is why, statistically, assonance, alliteration, and rhythm tend to be weaker in translations than in original texts; consciously or otherwise a writer, even of the least ambitious prose, is guided by sound, while the language itself is constantly forming standard collocations of words around pleasantly assonant combinations—fast asleep, wide awake. Any intervention in these patterns, whether simply substituting words to suit a local use of the same language, or, more radically, translating into another language, disturbs the relationship between sound and semantics.

But my train book isn't just a text written by an Englishman to be published in America. It's about Italy, the Italians, how they see things, their mental world. One of the ways one can get across the difference is to focus on words or usages that don't quite translate— the appearance of *coincidenza*, for example, in station announcements, which can mean a planned and timetabled train connection, or a quite unplanned, unexpected development to which an urgent response is required, such as a last-minute platform change. Over these matters the American editor dutifully followed. But where I had written *mamma* and *papà*, the edit had transformed to *mamma* and *pappa*. This rather threw me, in part because I had assumed that Americans said *mama* and *papa*, but mostly because *papà* is accented on the second syllable, whereas in Italian *pappa*, with the accent on the first syllable and that double *p* that Italians, unlike Anglo-Saxons, actually pronounce, is a word for mush, or baby food.

Despite my hailing from England—a country that still uses miles—I had expressed distances in meters and kilometers and it seemed odd now to find my Italian characters speaking to each other about yards and miles and, of course, Fahrenheit, which they never would. Or saying AM and PM, rather than using the twenty-four-hour clock as they mostly do, even in ordinary conversation. Slowly, as well as being concerned that some sentences were now feeling clunky and odd, I began to wonder if American readers really needed or demanded this level of protection. Wouldn't they soon figure out, if I said "the temperature was up in the sizzling thirties," that I was talking Celsius? Or at least that in another part of the world people had another system for measuring temperature according to which thirty was considered warm? Mightn't it be fascinating for them to be reminded that the twenty-four-hour clock, which Americans usually associate with military operations, has long been in standard civilian usage in Europe? Italy introduced it as early as 1893.

Or again, does a *newsagent* really need to become a *news dealer*, a *flyover* an *overpass*, a *parcel* a *package*, or in certain circumstances *between among* and *like such as*? Does the position of *also* really need to be moved in front of the verb *to be* in sentences like "Trains also were useful during the 1908 earthquake in Catania," when to me it looked much better after it? And does making these relatively small changes really make the text 100 percent American anyway? One thinks of how thoroughly the Harry Potter novels were Americanized for their US editions: would they really have sold fewer copies had the Anglicisms been kept? Wasn't half the charm of the series its rather fey Englishness (occasionally Scottishness)? Would we Americanize the Irish Joyce? Or again, if we want to have language conform to local usage, what about considering chronology as well as geography? Shouldn't we bring Dickens, Austen, Fielding, and Shakespeare up to date? Make it easier? Forget that language is constantly changing and different everywhere?

Turning page after page of the copy editor's notes, I began to make connections between this editing process and many of the things I have written about here. America is very much a net exporter of literature. Its novels are read and translated worldwide, where readers generally accept miles and Fahrenheit, pounds and ounces, AM and PM, and indeed have grown accustomed to these old-fashioned, American oddities (when it comes to doing science, of course, Americans use the more practical European systems). In Germany, for example, where around 50 percent of novels are foreign works in translation, Roth's and Franzen's characters are not obliged to discuss distances in kilometers.

Conversely, America imports very little—only 3 to 4 percent of novels published in the States are translations—and what it does import it tends to transform as far as possible into its own formulas and notations, in much the same way that Disney has turned every fable and myth worldwide into a version of Mickey Mouse. This situation is a measure of American power, but brings with it the danger of mental closure and inflexibility. Speaking recently at a conference in Milan, the Italian literary agent Marco Vigevani lamented that fewer and fewer American editors are able to read novels in Italian, French, and especially German, and this inevitably has reduced their enthusiasm for publishing foreign literature, since they are obliged to rely on external readers for advice.

Travel books are popular, likewise novels set in distant exotic countries, suggesting an appetite for awareness of other societies and their different lifestyles. But how far can literature really expose us to another world if everything is always returned to the reassuring medium of our own language *exactly as we use it*, with all our own formulas, dimensions, accents, and habits? More than anything else, what makes a foreign country foreign and difficult is its language, and though we can't be expected to learn a new language for every country we want to know about, it seems important to be reminded of the language, reminded that one's own language is not the supreme system for understanding the world, but just one of thousands of possibilities. Does anybody in the end really know with absolute certainty, all the differences between American and English usages? Aren't there a wide range of usages in both these countries? How can I know, when I see a particular edit, if it is an Americanism I have to accept, or a matter of individual taste I can take issue with?

And all this without mentioning house style, that frighteningly powerful dye which, in some magazines, turns every contributor's prose the same color. In my train book, for example, after a few pages discussing the fate of Italian railways under Nazi occupation, I begin a new paragraph "2,104 railwaymen died in the war": to my ear the bare number has exactly the brutal eloquence that such statements demand. But I find this changed to "A total of 2,104 railwaymen died in the Second World War." What is the sense of *a total of*? Surely it's not a requirement of Americanization. What does it add? I have to presume that some house style forbids me from opening a paragraph with a number. Why? This whole question may seem a quite different matter from the contrast between Americans Americanizing and Europeans accepting Americanisms, but the truth is that house style is a much more common occurrence in the US and more aggressively enforced, to the point that when one rereads work one has written for *The New Yorker* it no longer seems like one's own voice at all. I can think of no similar experience with English or European magazines, as I can remember no experience quite like my tussle over tense changes for the American edition of my book *Medici Money.*

Not that good editing is not precious. I have been saved a thousand stupid mistakes and much ugly phrasing by good editors; it is the desire to fix style in an unchanging standard that is noxious. As if people didn't have different ways of speaking. And a cultural trait like this must mean something, must come out of some deep assumption. Is it simply the publisher's anxiety that his readers are weak, ready to put their books down at the slightest obstacle, and hence must be reassured by a homogeneity of usage that more or less makes language invisible? Or could it be that the long American hegemony has bred an assumption that American formulations are inevitably global currency and should be universally imposed?

IN PRAISE OF THE LANGUAGE POLICE

HOW FAR SHOULD writers be asked to conform to standards of language and syntax? Behind this apparently innocent editorial dilemma lies the whole issue of what we expect from literature.

Most readers seem to favor (and indeed favour) complete freedom for writers, seeing nothing but pedantry in the application of rules and in some cases questioning whether such things can really be said to exist anywhere but in the heads of copy editors and the establishment police. As readers, it seems, we love to feel we are in direct contact with an especially creative, possibly subversive mind and that we are getting all of its quirks and qualities unmediated and unmitigated by the obtusity of lesser folks perversely eager to return everything to the expected and mundane. This is no doubt why so little is said about editing even in the more learned papers, while nothing at all appears in the popular press, let alone at a promotional level. One cannot imagine, for example, a publisher launching an advertising campaign to boast that it has the most attentive copy editors in the business and can guarantee that everything you may read from its list has been properly purged of anything grammatically iffy, or foreign, or idiosyncratic.

By the same token, very little is said of the mediating work of translators, even though we know that when a great piece of literature has been translated more than once, the various versions can sound quite different and obviously owe a great deal not just to the technical expertise but also to the personality and mindset of people we usually know nothing about. In general, we don't like to think of creative writing as a joint venture, and when it emerges, for example, that Raymond Carver allowed his work to be drastically edited, our appreciation of him, and indeed the work, is at least temporarily diminished. We want to think of our writers as geniuses occupying positions of absolute independence in relation to a tediously conventional society. Conversely, we abhor, or believe we abhor, the standard and the commonplace.

Yet nobody requires the existence of a standard and a general pressure to conform to that standard more than the person who wishes to assume a position outside it. It is essential for the creative writer that there be, or be perceived to be, a usual way of saying things, if a new or unusual way is to stand out and to provoke some excitement. So when D. H. Lawrence in *Women in Love* writes of Gudrun's insomnia after first making love to Gerald that she was "destroyed into perfect consciousness," he needs the reader to sense at once that this is syntactically anomalous; a person can be "transformed into," "turned into," "changed into" but not "destroyed into." The syntactical shock underlines Lawrence's unconventional view of consciousness as a negative rather than positive state, something that again is emphasized by the unexpected use of the word *perfect*,—"perfect consciousness"—rather than a more immediately understandable and neutral *intense.*

Naturally, anyone writing with this level of creativity needs a copy editor willing to accept that rules can be bent and broken. But that doesn't mean such editors have no role. It is important that the "special effect" stand out from a background of more conventional prose, and that a deliberate departure not be mistaken as something merely regional, British perhaps, or simply that there not be so much clutter around it of one kind or other that it is hardly noticed. George Orwell, a champion of strict grammar as a vehicle of clear thinking, memorably begins *1984* with a very simple, almost embarrassingly conventional novel-opener of a sentence in order that the anomaly constituted by the last word pack a big punch: "It was a bright cold day in April, and the clocks were striking thirteen." In a different field, David Hume, when presenting his radical and unconventional philosophy, did everything to remove from his writing any indication of his "Scottishness," sending drafts to friends to have them check his writing for "Scottishisms." It was not that he thought standard English superior, just that he did not want a reader's attention to be distracted from his main purpose.

The editor's job then becomes one of helping the writer to see where an unessential, perhaps unconscious departure from the norm is actually draining energy away from places where the text is excitingly unconventional. That is, the editor reminds an author that to construct a coherent identity he has to remember his relationship with society and with the language we share and cannot express ourselves without. To go out on a limb linguistically, accepting no compromise and creating an idiolect that really is entirely your own, may win awed admiration, as did *Finnegans Wake,* but will likely not attract many readers, and arguably does not allow for the communication of nuance, since all the ordinary reader will understand is that you are indeed off on a trip on your own; even Joyce's hitherto staunch supporter Pound, hardly a slouch himself when it came to literary experiments, would have no truck with it.

However, linguistic conventions, in so far as they exist and editors seek to apply them, tend to be national. Albeit with a degree of flexibility, the ear is accustomed to local patterns, and the eye has grown used to a certain system of punctuation, a certain approach to paragraphing (the *London Review of Books*, for example, is markedly different from *The New York Review of Books* in this regard). Hence the problem of what to do with a text from a different culture, a different country, a different language, or simply from the distant past, where any deliberate departures were intended to stand out against conventions that are not our own and that we very likely don't know or don't care about.

But if language habits tend to be national, we live in a world that is more and more international, a world where, certainly in Europe, readers are just as likely to be reading books in translation as in their national language. For translators, and indeed for editors of translations, there is a risk that they might not recognize the exciting subversiveness of a certain usage if they are not entirely familiar with the cultural standard and social context in which it is uttered: the first Italian translation of *1984* has the clocks striking one, not thirteen, its translator apparently unaware of how interesting a clock striking thirteen would be.

Even where translators and editors are sensitive to such effects, it may be impossible to achieve them within the different conventions of their own language. I have looked at translations of "destroyed into perfect consciousness" in many languages, and most of them split the structure into such formulas as "destroyed, absolutely aware." This is not because the translators are poor but because in their languages it is hard to find a standard usage ("transformed into") that can be bent to accept a word like *destroyed*, for the trick of Lawrence's expression is that its strangeness does not lead to a loss of fluency. Milan Kundera objected vigorously in *Testaments Betrayed* that his subversive formulations in Czech were returned, in translation, to standard German or French, but although it's true that translators and their editors are not always the most adventurous people, it is also the case that one language's rules are not another's.

All this alerts us to the fact that each text and each usage in the text has no absolute existence, content, or meaning, but is always understood in relation to where we are now, what we regularly read and expect to see on the page. The translator frequently finds himself obliged to translate not the words themselves, but the distance between those words and other words that might normally have been used, but weren't. It is a tough proposition.

Unless . . . unless we come to the conclusion that it no longer makes sense, or very soon may not make sense, to talk about different territories and rules and being "one of us." Very soon it may be that we are all, at least as far as literature is concerned, part of one global territory where we are obliged to be constantly aware of different customs not as if they were happening far away within fairly well-marked and self-contained boundaries, but as if they had become part of what happens on our street. In that case, we may, for a while, as international stylistic conventions slowly form, be obliged to accept that we live in an era of great confusion, where the exact position any writer is taking in relation to a presumed cultural standard has grown extremely problematic.

There is a fascinating moment in the history of translation that occurs sometime in the early twentieth century when, with some notable exceptions, translators stop translating the names of characters. It is as if Italian readers had become so aware of England that one could no longer go on talking of Niccolò Nickleby, Samuele Pickwick, and their famous author Carlo Dickens. Or you could say that the Christian name no longer suggests a parental choice and social reference that we can easily transfer into our own system of names, but rather an absolute unchangeable denotation of an individual. Charles Dickens is Charles Dickens throughout the universe.

In any event, this global mingling of cultures works against nuance and in favor of the loud, clamorous, highly stylized, and idiosyncratic voice that can stand out in the cosmopolitan crowd. It will be a world in which the need for an editor to mediate and clarify the position of the individual writer in relation to some hypothetical standard will be seriously challenged, but, in the general disorientation, all the more necessary. Indeed, it may well be that as the Internet era matures and more authors self-publish online without any editorial assistance, we will begin to grow nostalgic for those finicky copy editors who at least gave us something well-defined to kick against.

TRANSLATING IN THE DARK

"WE MUST BELIEVE in poetry translation, if we want to believe in World Literature." Thus Tomas Tranströmer, the Swedish poet and winner of the 2011 Nobel Prize in Literature, quoted in a recent essay by Robin Robertson, one of his translators. Robertson goes on to describe the difficulties of capturing Tranströmer's spare voice and masterful evocation of Swedish landscape in English, particularly if you don't know Swedish well. Robert Lowell, Robertson tells us, translated Tranströmer with only a "passing knowledge" of the language. Robertson himself describes a process wherein his Swedish girlfriend gives him a literal line-by-line translation into English, then reads the Swedish to him to give him "the cadences," after which he creates "relatively free" versions in English.

This approach to translation is not uncommon among poets (W. H. Auden gave us his versions of Icelandic sagas in much the same way). Nevertheless, Robertson feels the need to call on various authorities to sanction a translation process that assumes that poetry is made up of a literal semantic sense, which can easily be transmitted separately from the verse, and a tone, or music, which only a poet is sufficiently sensitive to reconstruct. Thus Robertson observes:

In his introduction to *Imitations* (1962), Robert Lowell writes that "Boris Pasternak has said that the usual reliable translator gets the literal meaning but misses the tone, and that in poetry tone is of course everything."

Here the "of course" skates over the fact that tone is always in relation to content: if the content were altered while diction and register remained the same, the tone would inevitably shift. One notes in passing the disparagement of the "usual reliable translator"—the fellow knows his foreign language, but doesn't understand poetry.

T. S. Eliot is then cited as having warned Lowell not to present his "imitations" of Tranströmer and others as "translations":

If you use the word translation in the subtitle it will attract all those meticulous little critics who delight in finding what seem to them mis-translations. You will remember all the fuss about Ezra Pound's Propertius.

Here collocating *meticulous* with *little* does the job that Lowell/Pasternak achieved with "usual reliable": there are always people who interfere but don't understand.

Robertson also calls on the British poet Jamie McKendrick, who, he feels, is "surely right" when he says "The translator's knowledge of language is more important than their knowledge of languages." How vague this remark is! Does it mean that the translator has one kind of knowledge of how language in general achieves its effects, and another of the nuts and bolts of the different languages he knows, the first kind being "more important" than the second? If that is the case, then to what degree more important? Wouldn't the two, rather, be interdependent and mutually sustaining? These perplexities apart, the thrust of McKendrick's argument is clear enough: we are sweeping aside the objection that a profound knowledge of a foreign language might be required to translate its poetry, or prose for that matter, thus clearing the path for a translation by someone who is an expert in the area that counts: our own language.

I really do not wish to nitpick. I enjoy Lowell's and Robertson's translations of Tranströmer, and Pound's Propertius. I am glad these people did the work they did, giving us many fine poems along the way. As a writer myself who has also done a number of translations I might be expected to have a vested interest in the idea that what skill I have in English sets me apart from the "usual reliable" translator. However, and quite regardless of whether we want to call such work translation or imitation, it does seem that a serious issue is being dispatched with indecent haste here.

Let us remember our most intense experiences of poetry in our mother tongue, reading Eliot and Pound as adolescents perhaps, Frost and Wallace Stevens, Auden and Geoffrey Hill, then coming back to them after many years, discovering how much more was there than we had imagined, picking up echoes of other literature we have read since, seeing how the poet shifted the sense of this or that word slightly, and how this alters the tone and feeling of the whole. And then let's also recall some of the finest poetry criticism we have read—by William Empson, Christopher Ricks, or Eliot himself—the ability of these men to fill in linguistic and literary contexts in such a way that the text takes on a deeper meaning, or to tease out relations inside a poem that had been obscure, but once mentioned are suddenly obvious and enrich our experience of the work.

Now imagine that, having a poet friend who wishes to translate these authors, you offer a literal translation of their poems in your second language, perhaps French, perhaps German, perhaps Spanish. Maybe you read *The Four Quartets* out loud, line by line, to give him the cadence. But does our translator friend, who doesn't know our language well, hear what we hear when we read aloud? The ono-matopoeia, perhaps. But a dying fall in one tongue may not be the same in another, not to mention the echoes of other texts, or simply of voices in the air in our language. During my thirty years in Italy I have often been told by uninitiated English friends what a beautiful and harmonious language Italian is; but that is Italian as heard by an ear accustomed to English sound patterns. To the Italian ear, and to mine these days, much of what is said in Italian grates. One hears the language differently when one knows it.

Why do those "usual reliable translators" often give us work that we feel is wooden or lackluster, thus inviting the poets to get in-volved? Teaching translation, I frequently deal with students who write well in their mother tongue, but whose translations into that tongue lack fluency. This brings us to a paradox at the heart of trans-lation: the text we take as inspiration is also the greatest obstacle to expression. Our own language prompts us in one direction, but the text we are trying to respect says something else, or says the same thing in a way that feels very different. All the same, what often frees the student to offer better translations is a deeper knowledge of the language he is working from: a better grasp of the original allows the translator to detach from formal structures and find a new expres-sion for the tone he is learning to feel: in this case, however, every departure from strict transposition is inspired by an intimate and direct experience of the original.

All this to arrive at the obvious conclusion that while expression and creativity in one's own language is crucial, a long experience in the language we are working from can only improve the translations we make. But the really interesting question is: Why are such intelli-gent writers as Eliot, Lowell, Pasternak, Robertson, and McKendrick unwilling to consider the matter more carefully? Is it because, to re-turn to Tranströmer, "We must believe in poetry translation, if we want to believe in World Literature"? There is no point, that is, in examining what we do too closely if we've already decided what we want our conclusion to be.

But why is it imperative that we believe in World Literature? It seems we must imagine that no literary expression or experience is ultimately unavailable to us; the single individual is not so conditioned by his own language, culture, and literature as not to be able to experience all other literatures; and the individual author likewise can be appreciated all over the globe. It is on this premise that all international literary prizes, of which there are now so many, depend. The zeitgeist demands that we gloss over everything that makes a local or national culture rich and deep, in order to believe in global transmission. There must be no limitation.

I have no quarrel with the aspiration, or all the intriguing translation/imitation processes it encourages. My sole objection would be that it is unwise to lose sight of the reality that cultures are immensely complex and different and that this belief in World Literature could actually create a situation where we become more parochial and bound in our own culture, bringing other work into it in a process of mere assimilation and deluding ourselves that, because it sounds attractive in our own language, we are close to the foreign experience. Tranströmer remarks:

> I perceived, during the first enthusiastic poetry years, all poetry as Swedish. Eliot, Trakl, Éluard—they were all Swedish writers, as they appeared in priceless, imperfect, translations.

Try this experiment: pick up a copy of a book mis-titled *Dante's Inferno*. It offers twenty celebrated poets, few of whom had more than a passing knowledge of Italian, each translating a canto of the *Inferno*. Inevitably, the result is extremely uneven as in each case we feel the Italian poet's voice being dragged this way and that according to each translator's assumptions of what he might or might not have sounded like. Sometimes it is Seamus Heaney's *Inferno*, sometimes it is Carolyn Forché's, sometimes it is W. S. Merwin's, but it is never Dante's. Then dip into the 1939 prose translation by the scholar John Sinclair. There is immediately a homogeneity and fluency here, a lack of showiness and a semantic cohesion over scores of pages that give quite a different experience. To wind up, look at Robert and Jean Hollander's 2002 reworking of Sinclair. Robert Hollander is a Dante scholar and has cleared up Sinclair's few errors. His wife, Jean, is a poet who, while respecting to a very large degree Sinclair's phrasing, has made some adjustments, under her husband's meticulous eye, allowing the translation to fit into unrhymed verse. It is still a long way from reading Dante in the original, but now we do feel that we have a very serious approximation and a fine read.

LISTENING FOR THE JABBERWOCK

WHAT IS THE status of translated works of literature? Are they essentially different from texts in their original form? One of the arguments I have put forward is that there is a natural tendency toward rhythm, alliteration, and assonance when one writes even the most ordinary prose, and that editing to conform to the linguistic conventions of a different culture can interfere with this. The translator gives priority to the semantic sense, but that sense was also partly guided in the original by what one might call the acoustic inertia of the language.

Naturally, an alert and resourceful translator can sometimes come up with the goods. Here for example is a sentence from Joyce's "The Dead":

It hardly pained him now to think how poor a part he, her husband, had played in her life.

A monosyllabic onslaught of p's and h's—the husband is the bisyllabic odd man out—falls into a melancholic, mostly iambic rhythm. A masterful Italian translation by Marco Papi and Emilio Tadini gives:

Ora non gli dava quasi più pena pensare a quanta poca parte lui, suo marito, aveva avuto nella sua vita.

The Italian inevitably settles for bisyllables but finds a host of *p*'s and a quiet, even rhythm to match the resigned tone of the English.

Such combinations of luck and achievement are rare, however, and mainly come in literary texts, poetry in particular, where the translator is prepared for the writer's evident and strategic use of poetic devices. All too often, the generous attempt to match such devices—one thinks of Pinsky's translation of the *Inferno*—only alert us to the strain and effort the translator has to make to force the language of translation into the desired sound patterns, patterns which in the original sounded easy and even natural. Meantime in novels, even the most evident poetic effects are often simply ignored. Here is D. H. Lawrence in *Women in Love* describing the combative Gudrun's encounter with an equally combative rabbit, Bismark:

> They unlocked the door of the hutch. Gudrun thrust in her arm and seized the great, lusty rabbit as it crouched still, she grasped its long ears. It set its four feet flat, and thrust back.

None of the translations I have looked at match Lawrence's repetition of *thrust* to suggest a parallel between the woman and the rabbit, the way the violence of the one provokes the response of the other and puts both on the same level. Nor do they capture the nice way the word *lusty* ties the two *thrusts* together soundwise: none of them begins to recover the stubbornness and economy of "set its four feet flat." It is not a question of poor translation; the text was created in English and that is that. This is what Paul Celan, despairing of translating Baudelaire, called "the fatal uniqueness of language," when the creative mind, deeply integrated within a set of native sound patterns, produces something that can exist exclusively in that language.

Another way of approaching the question of what is different about translation might be to look at a text where the usual relation between semantics and acoustic effects is radically altered. Everybody knows the opening of Lewis Carroll's "Jabberwocky":

> 'Twas brillig, and the slithy toves
> Did gyre and gimble in the wabe:
> All mimsy were the borogoves,
> And the mome raths outgrabe.

The comedy of the poem is its reproduction of a range of acoustic and rhythmic strategies that the reader immediately recognizes as typical of a certain kind of poetry, but with nonsense words. The suggestion is that all such poetry is driven to a degree by the inertia of style and convention, that the sound is as decisive as the sense in determining what gets said; indeed, when we "run out of sense," the sound trundles on of its own accord. But how could one begin to translate "mome raths outgrabe"? We have no idea what it means. The only strategy would be to find an equally hackneyed poetic form in the translator's language and play with it in a similar way.

Liberated by the fact that many of the words don't have any precise meaning, the translator should not find this impossible, though whether strictly speaking it is now a translation is another issue. Here is a heroic Italian version by Milli Graffi:

> *Era cerfuoso e i viviscidi tuoppi,*
> *Ghiarivan foracchiando nel pedano*
> *Stavano tutti mifri i vilosnuoppi,*
> *Mentre squoltian i momi radi invano.*

In general, however, what we find is a reproduction of the sense, but with a much diluted intensity of the Jabberwock effect. Developing Frost's notion that "poetry is what gets lost in translation," we might say that what we won't find in translation is this lively, often undiscriminating pattern of sounds, an ancient enchantment, which the best writers can integrate with their creativity and the worst simply allow to take over the show, as in the marvelously poor poetry of William McGonagall:

Beautiful Railway Bridge of the Silv'ry Tay!
Alas! I am very sorry to say
That ninety lives have been taken away
On the last Sabbath day of 1879,
Which will be remember'd for a very long time.

Translated texts, then, and there are ever more of them in the world today, tend to be cooler, a little less fluid—they will operate more on the rational intellect than on the rhythm-wired senses. They will deceive you less and charm you less. Of course there are notable exceptions, texts that were translated with the seduction of the reader and the beauty of the language very much in mind. Where these are old and central to our culture—the Bible, most obviously—they can become canonical on a par with our homegrown writing. But there are remarkably few of them.

I have often wondered if that is why, in certain countries, translations now even seem to be preferred to works written in the native language. A large study carried out at my university on four corpuses of texts—Italian novels before 1960, English novels translated into Italian before 1960, Italian novels after 1990, and English novels translated into Italian after 1990—suggests that while the national language in Italy is changing fast, with Italian novelists ever more open to stylistic influence from the cinema or from abroad, translations into Italian keep alive a hypercorrect literary Italian that has otherwise lapsed into disuse. Even the most disturbing texts can, at least linguistically, deprived of the Jabberwock effect, prove calm and reassuring.

IN THE WILDS OF LEOPARDI

I'M STARTING A translation, my first for many years, and at once I'm faced with the fatal, all-determining decision: What voice do I translate this in?

Usually one would say: the same voice as the original's, as you hear it in the Italian and imagine it in English. This would be along the line of Dryden's famous injunction to translators to write as the author would write if he were English—a rather comical idea since we are interested in the author largely because he comes from elsewhere and does not write like an Englishman. In any event, this text is a special case.

I'm translating a selection of entries from Giacomo Leopardi's *Zibaldone*. This is a book all Italians know from school though almost nobody has read it in its entirety. The word *zibaldone* comes from the same root as *zabaione* and originally had the disparaging sense of a hotchpotch of food, or any mixture of heterogeneous elements, then a random collection of notes, a sort of diary, but of disconnected thoughts and reflections rather than accounts of events. Leopardi, born in 1798 and chiefly remembered for his lyric poetry, kept his *Zibaldone* from 1817 to 1832, putting together a total of 4,526 handwritten pages. Printed editions come in at something over two thousand pages, before the editor's notes, which are usually many. There is general agreement that the *Zibaldone* is one of the richest mines of reflection on the modern human condition ever written. Schopenhauer in particular referred to Leopardi as "my spiritual brother" and saw much of his own thinking foreshadowed in Leopardi's writings, though he had never seen the *Zibaldone*, which at the time was still unpublished. The selection I'm translating, put together by an Italian publisher, is made up of all the entries that Leopardi himself had flagged as having to do with feelings and emotions.

Immediately two problems arise as far as establishing a voice for translation. First, the book is almost two hundred years old; second, even if Leopardi might have imagined its being published, it was certainly not written or prepared for publication and is full of elisions, abbreviations, notes to himself, rewrites, and cross-references. In fact, on his death in 1837 the huge wad of pages was dumped in a trunk by his friend Antonio Ranieri and was not published in its entirety until 1900. So, do I write in modern prose, or in an early-nineteenth-century pastiche? Do I tidy up the very personal and unedited aspect of the text, or do I preserve those qualities, if I can?

The first question would be more tormented if I felt I had any ability to write an approximation of early-nineteenth-century English. I don't. So that's that. But I'm also suspicious of the very idea of such time parallels. English and Italian were in very different phases of development in the 1830s. Official English usage had largely been standardized in the previous century, and novelists like Dickens were preparing to launch a full-scale assault on that standardization. Not to mention the fact that American English already had a very different feel than British English. Meantime, Italian hardly existed as a national language. Only around 5 percent of Italians were actually speaking and reading Italian when the country achieved political unification in 1861. The literary language, dating back to Petrarch, Dante, and Boccaccio, was Tuscan, and this is the language Leopardi writes in, but without ever having been to Tuscany, at least when he began the *Zibaldone*. For him, it's a very mental, cerebral language, learned above all from books. Does it make any sense to move from this to the language of Shelley and Byron, or Emerson and Hawthorne?

Even given these circumstances, Leopardi was special to the point of idiosyncrasy. Brought up in a provincial town in the Papal State of central Italy, then one of the most backward territories in Europe, son of an eccentric aristocrat fallen upon hard times, Leopardi was a prodigy who seems to have spent his whole childhood in his father's remarkable library. By age ten he had mastered Latin, Greek, German, and French. Hebrew and English would soon follow. The *Zibaldone* is peppered with quotations from these languages, and they can be heard, particularly the Latin, here and there in his prose. Thinking aloud, as he seeks to turn intuition and reflection into both a history of the human psyche and a coherent but very private philosophy of nihilism (with his own shorthand terms, which sometimes don't quite mean what standard usage would suppose them to mean), he latches on to any syntax that comes his way to keep the argument moving forward. Some sentences are monstrously long and bizarrely assembled, shifting from formal structures to the most flexible use of apposition, juxtaposition, inference, and implication. The one other translation of an "old" text I have done, Machiavelli's *The Prince*, was a picnic by comparison.

Do I keep the long sentences, then, or break them up? Do I make the book more comprehensible for English readers than it is for present-day Italian readers (for whom footnotes giving a modern

Italian paraphrase are often provided)? Above all, do I allow all those Latinisms to come through in the English, which would inevitably give the text a more formal, austere feel, or do I go for Anglo-Saxon monosyllables and modern phrasal verbs to get across the curiously excited intimacy of the text, like someone building up very complex, often provocative ideas as he goes along, with no one at hand to demand explanations or homogeneity or any sort of order?

Here, for example, is a brief and by Leopardi's standards very simple entry on hope and suicide:

> *La speranza non abbandona mai l'uomo in quanto alla natura. Bensì in quanto alla ragione. Perciò parlano stoltamente quelli che dicono (gli autori della Morale universelle t.3.) che il suicidio non possa seguire senza una specie di pazzia, essendo impossibile senza questa il rinunziare alla speranza ec. Anzi tolti i sentimenti religiosi, è una felice e naturale, ma vera e continua pazzia, il seguitar sempre a sperare, e a vivere, ed è contrarissimo alla ragione, la quale ci mostra troppo chiaro che non v'è speranza nessuna per noi. [23. Luglio 1820.]*

Do I write:

> Hope never abandons man in relation to his nature, but in relation to his reason. So people (the authors of *La morale universelle*, vol. 3) are stupid when they say suicide can't be committed without a kind of madness, it being impossible to renounce all hope without it. Actually, having set aside religious sentiments, always to go on hoping is a felicitous and natural, though true and continuous, madness and totally contrary to reason which shows too clearly that there is no hope for any of us. [July 23, 1820]

Or alternatively:

> Men never lose hope in response to nature, but in response to
> reason. So people (the authors of the *Morale universelle*, vol. 3)
> who say no one can kill themselves without first sinking into
> madness, since in your right mind you never lose hope, have got
> it all wrong. Actually, leaving religious beliefs out of the equa-
> tion, our going on hoping and living is a happy, natural, but
> also real and constant madness, anyway quite contrary to rea-
> son which all too clearly shows that there is no hope for any of
> us. [July 23, 1820]

Or some mixture of the two? The fact is that while I find it hard to
imagine translating Dante's famous *Lasciate ogni speranza* any
other way than "Abandon all hope" (curiously introducing this
rather heavy verb, *abandon*, where in the Italian we have a simple
lasciare, to leave), here I just can't imagine any reason for not reorga-
nizing *La speranza non abbandona mai l'uomo* into "Man never
loses hope."

And if I leave dangling modifiers like "having set aside religious
sentiments," am I going to find an editor intervening as if I'd simply
made a mistake? If I warn the editor that there will be dangling modifiers because Leopardi doesn't worry about them, does that mean
that I can then introduce them myself where Leopardi doesn't?

All these decisions are further complicated by the fact that as I
began my translation of two hundred pages of extracts, a team of
seven translators, and two specialist editors, based in Birmingham,
England, and largely sponsored by, of all people, Silvio Berlusconi,
completed the first unabridged and fully annotated English edition of
the *Zibaldone*, a simply enormous task. Their version had not yet
been published at this point (by Farrar, Straus and Giroux in the

United States) but I had a proof copy. Do I look at it? Before I start? Or only after I finish, to check that at least semantically we have understood the same thing?

Well, certainly the latter and with due acknowledgement of course; there is absolutely no point in my publishing a version with mistakes that could have been avoided by checking my attempt against theirs, as quite possibly they will have been checking theirs against the recent French version. On the other hand, there is equally no point in my producing a translation that is merely an echo of theirs. I'd be wasting my time. This kind of translation just doesn't pay enough for you not to need some other incentive: the crumb of glory that might accrue from producing a memorable Leopardi.

I decide to look at the Translator's Note in the new edition, and perhaps a few parts of the translation that don't correspond to the extracts I'm supposed to be translating, just to get a sense of how they've dealt with the various issues of style. Immediately I realize that these translators faced an even greater dilemma than I do. Seven translators and two editors will each have heard Leopardi's highly idiosyncratic voice and responded to his singular project, his particular brand of despair, in his or her own way; but one can't publish a text with seven (or nine) different voices. Strategies must have been agreed on, and a single editor must ultimately have gone through all two-thousand-plus pages to even things out. This means establishing a standard voice that all the translators can aim for and making certain decisions across the board, particularly with respect to key words, the overall register, lexical fields, and so on. In any event, after reading a few paragraphs of the translation itself I'm reassured that my work will not merely be a duplication of theirs, because I hear the text quite differently.

Here the reader will want me to characterize this difference, perhaps with a couple of quotations. And the temptation would be for me to show something I could criticize and to draw the reader onto my side to support some supposedly more attractive approach. But I don't want to do that. I'm frankly in awe of the hugeness of this team's accomplishment and aware that they have done things the only way they could to offer a complete translation of the whole text.

What I'd rather like to stress is my intense awareness, as I read their translation, of each reader's response, which is the inevitable result, I suppose, of the individual background we bring to a book, all the reading and writing and listening and talking we've done in the past, our particular interests, beliefs, obsessions. I hear the writer in an English that has a completely different tone and feel than the one that emerges from my colleague's collective efforts. It's just a different man speaking to me—a different voice—though the Leopardi I hear is no more valid than the Leopardi—or Leopardis—they hear.

ECHOES FROM THE GLOOM

FIFTEEN YEARS OF diary entries. From 1817 to 1832. Some just a couple of lines. Some maybe a thousand words. At a rhythm ranging from two or three a day to one a month, or even less frequent. Suddenly, it occurs to me that if Leopardi were writing his *Zibaldone* today, it would most likely be a blog. Immediately, the thought threatens to affect the way I am translating the work. I am imagining the great diary as the *Ziblogone*—the big blog—launched from some eccentric little website in the hills of central Italy. I'm wondering if I should suggest to the publishers (Yale University Press) that they might put the entries up one a day on their site; they could use Leopardi's own system of cross-referencing his ideas to create a series of links. Fantastic! Perhaps I could start embedding the links as I work. Why not?

It is impossible to translate a work from the past and not be influenced by what has happened since. Or at least to feel that influence, if only to resist it. I translated Machiavelli's *The Prince* during the Iraq War. States invading distant foreign countries with authoritarian governments, Machiavelli warned, should think twice about disbanding the army and bureaucracy that opposed them, since these institutions may offer the best opportunity of maintaining law and order after the war is over. I remember wanting to translate this observation in such a way that even the obtuse Mr. Bush simply could not miss the point. If I could have sneaked in the word *Iraq*—or perhaps more feasibly *shock* and *awe*—I would have.

With Leopardi, there are no problems of this kind. Nor does he have the sort of reputation that might prompt a translator to work toward a text that people are expecting. Although Italians consider him one of their greatest writers, Leopardi is hardly known in the Anglo-Saxon world, apart from his poetry (Jonathan Galassi published a translation of Leopardi's complete poetic works as recently as 2011). However, even in Italy there is a staunch resistance to his prose work and philosophical thinking. It is not merely because he is ferociously anticlerical that so many "polite" thinkers shy away, or seek to disqualify him—Mazzini and Garibaldi were if possible even more so, but remain popular for their political positivism. There is also his absolutely lucid and quite remorseless pessimism. Here he is, in a fairly light moment, talking about universal envy:

> The sight of a happy man, full of some good luck he's had, or even just moderately cheered by it, some promotion won or favor granted, etc., is almost always extremely irksome not just to people who are upset or depressed, or simply not prone to joyfulness, whether out of choice or habit, but even to people neither happy nor sad and not at all harmed or deflated by this success. Even when it comes to friends and close relatives it's the same. So that the man who has reason to be happy will either have to hide his pleasure, or be casual and amusing about it, as if it hardly mattered, otherwise his presence and conversation will prove hateful and tiresome, even to people who ought to be happy about his good luck or who have no reason at all to be upset by it. This is what thoughtful, well-educated people

do, people who know how to control themselves. What can all this mean but that our self-regard inevitably and without our noticing leads us to hate our fellow man? There's no doubt that in situations like this, even the nicest people with nothing at all to gain or lose from another's success, will need to get a grip on themselves and show a certain heroism to join in the partying, or merely not to feel depressed by it.

How does this cosmic pessimism, as it's sometimes called, affect my translation? As one reads the *Zibaldone*, one can't help feeling that one has heard its voice elsewhere. Either Leopardi has had more influence than I knew about, or others since have arrived at similar combinations of gloomy content and emphatic style. An Italian can't help thinking of Giorgio Manganelli and Carlo Emilio Gadda. But the voices that for me are most constantly present, or nascent, in long sections of the *Zibaldone*, are Samuel Beckett's (the novels), Emil Cioran's, and, above all—indeed overwhelmingly, especially in the wilder riffs on the scandals of human behavior—Thomas Bernhard's. This is Bernhard's character Reger in *Old Masters* reflecting on the value of painting:

Art altogether is nothing but a survival skill, we should never lose sight of this fact, it is, time and again, just an attempt — an attempt that seems touching even to our intellect — to cope with this world and its revolting aspects, which, as we know, is invariably possible only by resorting to lies and falsehoods, to hypocrisy and self-deception, Reger said. These pictures are full of lies and falsehoods and full of hypocrisy and self-decep-tion, there is nothing else in them if we disregard their often inspired artistry. All these pictures, moreover, are an expres-sion of man's absolute helplessness in coping with himself and with what surrounds him all his life. That is what all these pictures express, this helplessness which, on the one hand, embarrasses the intellect and, on the other hand, bewilders the same intellect and moves it to tears, Reger said.

So, how far should I allow this perception of affinity to influence the way I translate? Can I prevent it? Am I just reading Bernhard back into Leopardi, or is the style, the attitude, really there in the *Zibaldone*? I'm sure it is. Beckett certainly had read Leopardi, as had Cioran, but Bernhard? Bernhard was influenced by Beckett, occasionally to the point of plagiarism, and by Cioran of course. And he would have read Schopenhauer, who felt a great affinity for Leopardi, though Schopenhauer couldn't have read the *Zibaldone* itself, since it wasn't published until long after his death. Still, the more I think about it the less it matters whether Bernhard had actually read Leopardi or not. What is at stake here is the way a certain optimistic Christian socialism that has dominated in the West, an attitude that relies heavily on denial—benign denial, one might call it—has naturally spawned its opposite in writers whose fierce rhetoric determinedly exposes every illusion.

If, as a translator, I focus entirely on the semantics and the order in which Leopardi's sentences are set up—something that the translators of the complete *Zibaldone*, shortly to be published by Farrar, Straus and Giroux, have tended to do, in understandable respect of the rigor of the writer's thought—then that rhythm of scandal that I am hearing in his prose, the need to insist, against the grain of all conformity, that things really are as bad as they can be, the world a "solid nothing" and man, particularly modern man, "utterly beyond all hope"—will largely be lost. Because an insistent rhythm in English is not created the same way as it is in Italian, and because Leopardi's sentences have such a determined flow, pushing forward impatiently, but remorselessly, with frequent repetitions and redundancies and constant lists that suddenly break off in edgy etceteras (my Word software counts 8,738 of them in the *Zibaldone*). Here he is talking about the near impossibility of sincere friendship between those of the same profession:

> For example, accepted that perfect friendship, abstractly considered, is impossible and contradictory to human nature, between peers even ordinary friendship becomes extremely difficult, rare and inconstant, etc. Schiller, a man of great feeling, was hostile to Goethe (since not only are people of the same profession not friends with each other, or less friendly, but there is actually more hatred between them than between others who are not in the same circumstances) etc. etc. etc.

As I see it, there would be little point in getting the semantics absolutely right, and even readable, if one failed to convey this emotive, Bernhardesque urgency; for, crucially, the emphatic rhythm—the hyperbole and insistence with which the pessimism is delivered—both increases its impact, and becomes its consolation, almost its comedy. Leopardi is not unaware of the perverse pleasure one can take in having demonstrated how bad things are. One of the passages that most gets me thinking of Bernhard, and resisting him, begins with a quote from the *Aeneid* where Virgil has Queen Dido declaring she will die unavenged, but is happy to die all the same. Leopardi reflects:

> Here Virgil wanted to get across (and it's a deep, subtle sentiment, worthy of a man who knew the human heart and had experience of passion and tragedy) the pleasure the mind takes in dwelling on its downfall, its adversities, then picturing them for itself, not just intensely, but minutely, intimately, completely;

in exaggerating them even, if it can (and if it can, it certainly will), in recognizing, or imagining, but definitely in persuading itself and making absolutely sure it persuades itself, beyond any doubt, that these adversities are extreme, endless, boundless, irremediable, unstoppable, beyond any redress, or any possible consolation, bereft of any circumstance that might lighten them; in short in seeing and intensely feeling that its own personal tragedy is truly immense and perfect and as complete as it could be in all its parts, and that every door towards hope and consolation of any kind has been shut off and locked tight, so that now he is quite alone with his tragedy, all of it. These are feelings that come in moments of intense desperation as one savors the fleeting comfort of tears (when you take pleasure supposing yourself as unhappy as you can ever be), sometimes even at the first moment, the first emotion, on hearing the news, etc., that spells disaster, etc.

What Leopardi has that Bernhard hasn't is the glorious understatement of that final *etcetera*, which diminishes the particular drama, and dramatically worsens the human plight.

MY NOVEL, THEIR CULTURE

HOW SHOULD A novelist feel on seeing his work translated, completely, into not just another medium, but also another culture?

Recently, I opened a DVD package with the title *Stille* (Silence), put it into my computer, and sat down to watch. Actually, I had received this DVD a month earlier. It is an Austrian film production of my novel *Cleaver*. I did not look at it at once because I was in denial. I have been generously paid for the rights to film, I am delighted it has been made and grateful to the producer for pushing it through, but *Cleaver* was written in English and has an English hero from a specific milieu—a journalist and documentary filmmaker who, as the book opens, has carried out, for the BBC, a destructive interview of an American president easily recognizable as George Bush.

It would be nice (for me) to have an English or American film adaptation of the book—or at least a version in the English language. But the DVD was sent to me in German with no subtitles, and my German isn't great. That is my fault, of course, not the producer's. It would make no sense for the Austrian production company to dub or subtitle the film, if it doesn't have a potential English-language buyer. Its target market is German national TV.

The idea of the novel is simple: Harold Cleaver, sensual, in his

fifties, an overweight womanizer, witty and worldly-wise, at the top
of his journalistic game, is profoundly shocked by a novelized family
biography written by his son, Alex, which reveals him, Cleaver, as a
bully, a megalomaniac, utterly insensitive to his partner, the boy's
mother, and largely responsible for the death of Angela, Alex's talented rock-singer sister. Cleaver's ire and dismay on reading this are
partly responsible for the ferocity of his interview with the US president, but also his decision, immediately afterward, on the opening
page of the novel, to abandon London, his family, journalism, everything he knows, and escape to a place where he, a great communica-
tor, can't speak to anyone and where no one will recognize him: the
Italian South Tyrol.

Living in Verona, I am close to South Tyrol, which has always
been a holiday destination for me; after thirty years here I know it
well. In the high Alpine valleys, its sparse population speaks a German dialect that even many Germans and Austrians find hard to
understand. On arrival Cleaver proceeds to look for a place, as he
puts it, above the noise line, high up in the mountains, where there is
no reception for his cell phone, no electricity, no means of communication at all. He wants to cut himself off, perhaps to die. Eventually,
he rents a tiny hut, Rosenkrantzhof, his only contact a peasant family
with whom he has to communicate in sign language. Alone in the
vast alpine emptiness, he discovers that the mind grows louder and
more frightening when the world around is silent. As winter deepens
and physical survival becomes an issue, Cleaver cannot free himself
from an interminable, mentally exhausting quarrel with his son's
book, and a growing awareness of how completely his main life
choices, indeed his entire consciousness, have been driven by the fe-
verish media environment he lived in, a certain way of thinking, talking, and exhibiting oneself, with which we are all familiar.

In the film everything is rearranged. Rightly so. Film must use different tools to unpack the same can of worms. The opening image, as the titles go up, is a mountain swept by a blizzard. A figure emerges from a hut on an exposed ridge and trudges, staggers into snow-drifts, falls, and lies still. This scene anticipates the story's climax when Cleaver almost perishes in the snow. A voiceover cuts in; it is the son narrating from his book. However, my eye was captured by the long list of German names appearing on the screen: Jan Fedder, Iris Berben, Florian Bartholomäi, Anna Fischer. And then, very much the odd man out, Tim Parks. Gratifying, but displaced. I'm aware of course that it is the novel's setting in a German-speaking world, in a territory that was once an Austrian possession, that has made it possible for the Austrian producer to raise the necessary funds to make the film. By lucky accident my setting fits in perfectly with certain Austrian, German, and European regulations for obtaining public finance for filmmaking.

Cut to Cleaver as TV talk-show host. He is a German Cleaver. German face—the jowls, the hairstyle—German suit, German body language, and behind him one of those urban backdrops they like to put behind TV announcers to suggest that they are in the center of urban bustle and not buried deep in the stale corridors of a TV studio. The backdrop is a broad canal, or waterway, at night, with handsome, brightly lit white buildings on either side, monuments, distant traffic, cafés. The German or Austrian viewer will doubtless know where this is. Vienna perhaps? Or Berlin? Or Hamburg? I just don't know. But immediately I feel they have done the right thing, Germanizing everything. The German-speaking audience must recognize the media world that the German Cleaver operates in, the world they see on their news programs every night. But I realize that even if they dub or subtitle the film, my own English friends will not have the same sense of immersion they would get if the backdrop were London, the people Londoners.

I wonder if this Cleaver has an Austrian accent. Surely not, if the Austrians are aiming at German TV. I put the actor's name in Google and find he is from Hamburg. I wonder why they have kept the name Cleaver, pronounced exactly as in the English, but now spelt Cliewer, in line with German phonetics, and transformed into Harry Cliewer rather than the more sober, at least in English, Harold Cleaver. Though I chose it spontaneously, instinctively, the word/name Cleaver came to be important for me as I progressed with the novel for its anti-thetical semantic energies, the idea of cleaving *to* someone (in marriage, in oneness), and splitting something away from something else: Is Cleaver irreversibly attached to his family and milieu or can he really split away from them and become someone new and different? Is the mind free to leave the culture that formed it? Those were the thoughts going through my mind as I described his flight, then his disappointment that moving away has only intensified his mental belonging. The cover to the DVD shows Cliewer face-on raising an axe above his head, but the connection with his name—axe, cleaver—is lost, and anyway the German title for the printed novel is *Stille*, silence.

Five minutes in and here comes the big scene with George Bush, shortly before the 2004 election. (As I wrote the book I wasn't sure whether Bush would be re-elected or not; nor was Cleaver as he escaped the Tyrol—it's one of the things he thinks about in his isolation.) But no, the film doesn't give us the American president. It would hardly be conceivable that the American president would submit to an interview on the German *Harry Cliewer Show*, as he might perhaps submit to the most senior BBC journalist on a program with the more serious name of *Crossfire*. Through the clanking of my rusty German, I appreciate that this villain is a banker. The film has been updated and localized to bring us to the recent European banking crisis and the Euro emergency. This is very smart. German viewers will appreciate Cliewer's kamikaze courage in taking on the head of the Bundesbank—is that who he is?—in what is to be his last interview. Cleaver—sorry, Cliewer (I have checked the name in German dictionary to see if it exists as a word, but there is no trace of it) throws down a handful of five-hundred-euro notes on his desk and makes some insulting remark, at which the banker, who clearly expected an easier ride, stands up and stalks out in fury.

I am struck by this thought: had the movie been made by a British or American company and the original scenario—Cleaver versus Bush—been retained, or perhaps moved to an American rather than British setting, European viewers would have had no problem picking up a London or, say, Washington backdrop. They would immediately have recognized the American president and appreciated what was at stake. All over the world, people have seen so many American and British movies that even the milieu would have been superficially familiar. Many of them would have had no problem watching the movie in English, and watching a movie in a foreign language always leaves one feeling pleased with oneself for having acquired that language. In other words, the simple fact that I'm British, from London, with a familiarity with that milieu—Cleaver himself is based on a London journalist I know well—gave my novel a more global potential. It could have worked in Germany without these changes.

However, in order to get public funding, the Austrian filmmakers had to set the work in German-speaking Europe, indeed largely in the Tyrol (the Austrian, not the Italian Tyrol). And anyway they no doubt and very rightly feel far more at home making the work local and specific to their community, since as I have said it is to be broadcast on TV and not, so far as I know, released in cinemas around the world. As a result they have made a product that even if dubbed would not so easily appeal to an international market. My feeling is that the producers have done absolutely the right thing both aesthetically and given the production situation in which they must operate. But the megalomaniac Parks would have preferred his name in cinemas across the globe.

The strangest transformation, though, comes with the Tyrol. The protagonist of the novel is a man from a familiar, highly nuanced London setting, the center, as the British see it, of Anglo-Saxon news media—London interiors, London furniture, recognizably London banter. He is shifted to a place that is essentially, nowhere, a mountain waste, in late fall, people who are quite incomprehensible (the novel—a medium made up of words—has unexplained lines in South Tyrolese dialect); interiors that are generically antique, peasant, and Teutonic. It's so disconnected from everything Cleaver knows that he struggles to see it as anything but caricature, struggles to understand that the few people he meets are indeed real people with real lives who, despite not being at the center of the media world, deserve attention and respect.

Instead and inevitably, for German and Austrian viewers, the Alps, the Tyrol are very much part of their familiar world and mental landscape. Cliewer has no trouble understanding people there, and indeed barely a day or two after his arrival, a local newspaper has his photo on the front page, so everyone recognizes him. This introduces whole areas of reflection and perhaps significant German material that could not be in my book. This may make the film a richer experience for the German public, at least in this sense, though it entirely sacrifices the drama of Cleaver's not only going somewhere very remote, but above all divesting himself of his main strength, his language.

I watch the film unfold with a mixture of admiration, bewilderment, and, for purely selfish and private reasons, disappointment. My potentially global work has been made local. It is now locked into Germanic culture. It portrays the German media world, a distinctly German sensuality, a concrete Tyrolese. Well, haven't I written frequently in admiration of the artist happy to engage with his local community and ignore the global? Indeed I have. But this local is not my local. And of course, thanks to the complex laws of film rights and copyright, something else I have recently expressed a few opinions about, it will now not be easy for English or American producers to make their own version of the film. Like it or not, Cleaver, *Cleaver*, really has expatriated. He's Cliewer now.

Tim Parks has written seventeen novels, including *Europa*, which was short-listed for the Booker Prize, and most recently, *Painting Death*. He is the author of several works of non-fiction, including *Italian Neighbors* and *Italian Ways*. Parks has also translated the works of Alberto Moravia, Giacomo Leopardi, and Niccolò Machiavelli, among others, and he is a frequent contributor to *The New York Review of Books* and the *London Review of Books*. He lives in Italy.